RIGHT TO LIFE

RIGHT TO LIFE

A HUMAN RIGHTS ANTHOLOGY

Edited by
Kelly Esparza

FP

FOLKWAYS PRESS, LLC

Texas, USA
www.folkwayspress.com

Right to Life first published in 2024

Printed and bound in the United States by
IngramSpark

ISBN: 978-1-7362701-3-4

9 8 7 6 5 4 3 2 1

CONTENTS

RIGHT TO LIFE

POETRY

A LETTER TO MY ADULT DIAGNOSIS

by Amberlynn Gonzales

Hello, to the parent I didn't know I had
Nice to meet you, you who reared me,
Watered me, and tended to me with
Procrastination and "poor time management skills"

You make it so hard to function
Hard for the cogs in my head
To connect and revolve
For this revolution inside me
to turn outward to action

I want to turn the channel on this static body
And channel this heart into energy
It's so easy for you to go unseen,
Blend into the background as white noise

The problem is that the solution
Is the only evident part of the equation
i is an (f), function, if you erase
All my attempts at functioning

My wild wide pendulum swings
From inability to do anything I need to do
All the way to sleepless nights finishing
My neglected necessary to-dos

Now all my fuses have been blown
You plunge me into dark with winter
But though the seasons change,
Still I find I can't spring into motion

These coils are too covered in rust
And I'm running into a crash
Running a company called Dysfunction
Where I am the Chief Executive

But my mom raised me too
And never taught me how to fail
Medication or depression
I will not shy from facing the world

I'm a machine that's all heart and no drive
And sometimes machines need maintenance
So, if you break me down, beware
Because my dad raised a mechanic

Amberlynn Gonzales (she/he/they) is a queer Chicanx poet hailing from West Texas whose work largely explores identity, love, and trauma. They have showcased their poetry in local festivals and events including East Lubbock Art House's Voices of East Lubbock and Lubbock's North by Northeast.

ABLEISM'S FOOTHOLD

by Simon Quinn

Ableism creeps
Slowly into crevices
And whispers its lies
Into ears that bracket empty heads.

Employers who watch you collapse
Instead of follow the law
Mistake their hatred for kindness
As they "let you go."
Their argument, "unfairness."
To the others though, not me.
Apparently sitting is unethical.

Ableism seeps
Slithering into spaces
Growing in the cracks
That no one cares to fill,
Only cover with false promises.

They tell you
They care about equality
While silently only meaning it
If you:
Look the same
Speak the same
Walk the same as them.

Ableism bleeds
Pumping out the instinct
To agree it's my fault.
Letting only tears
Escape the pounding of my head,

Accommodations are *not* special treatment.
The ADA is *not* a suggestion.
My bones don't follow the whims
Of people who don't constantly ache.

Simon Quinn is a proud graduate of Northern Arizona University. He delighted in studying subjects that could help him tell better puns: English, Creative Writing, and Geology. As a disabled, queer writer, his poetry is often about his life experiences and his fiction focuses on representing people like him. In his free time he enjoys playing with his extremely fluffy cat and collecting heart-shaped rocks. You can find him on Instagram at spellboundqueer.

YOU DON'T SEEM AUTISTIC

(GETHSEMANE)

by Noah Fischbach

But I alone
witnessed the brief
serenity
          after whistling a nasal soliloquy
          that purified my brain like
cocaine. I was my own drug,
     plastering the unknowing folk
     with

pulsating, hexadecimal-bullshit-calculations that
     only I could crack.
I knew the answer to everything lay hidden just
     beneath the flaking, crisp
crust–

to some, dissipated like butter into nether
earth, and to others, springs filled to bursting
from which
the left-handed
discovered autonomy.

My mind wanders deserts
far greater than
yours; solitudinal
fortresses of liminal spaces and
passionately inverted
angles
threatened by grease-slick sentences
and ninety-degree diagrams. A pint of mercy
granted
since hidden executions began
now
runneth
over;
normalcy forbidden in the name of
genderful God.
Unconsenting consciousness begets
birthmark symbol of
dichotomic deity.

Three and a half years ago–I am Christ
in Gethsemane–hands trembling,

carpenter's cup raised to bloody lips,
finger-thimble-moment by moment
awaiting an uncertain morning.

Noah Fischbach (he/him) is a senior at Capital University in Columbus, Ohio. He has been previously published in *Tomorrow and Tomorrow*, *Ekstasis*, and *ReCap*. He is currently pursuing a research project concerning the effects of participatory media culture on the neurodiverse community. He is an ardent *Star Trek* fan and enjoys spending time with close friends.

UNTHINKABLE

by Donia Hanaei

She is being dragged away.
Once she is in the green and white car,
    who knows when she'll be seen again?
If she will be seen again.
Her crime was unthinkable.
At least 70 lashes.
She let her hair float on the wind.

He is being dragged away.
Once he is in the green and white car,
    who knows if he'll ever be the same?
If he survives.
His crime was unthinkable;
He will hang for it.
He loved a man.

He is being dragged away.
Once he is in the green and white car,
who knows how he will return?
If he will return.
His crime was unthinkable;
Both hands must be severed.
He took naan for his children.

She is being dragged away.
Once she is in the green and white car,
who knows when she will wake up?
If she wakes up.
Her crime was unthinkable;
She had the potential to resist.
Just a schoolgirl sitting in class.

They are being dragged away.
Once they are in the ambulance the basij have
seized, they have little chance of return.
Maybe their mothers will get their bodies.
Their crimes were unthinkable;
They answered with their lives.
Bodies tortured and mangled that dared to
demand freedom.

Donia Hanaei is an Iranian-American living in the Southern United States and bringing awareness to civil and human rights violations in the United States and the Middle East. As an outspoken Iranian woman, she is unable to return to Iran so long as the current authoritarian regime exists; returning risks imprisonment or worse. Donia works in the nonprofit and civil rights space where she seeks to provide in-language resources to communities in need including but not limited to civic engagement resources, legal services, interpreter sessions and more. She holds a Bachelor of Arts in International Affairs with an emphasis on the Middle East and North Africa from the University of Colorado Boulder and a Master of Arts in International Relations from the University of North Georgia.

BLACK WOMAN

by Amari Pollard

I am in love with you,
Black Woman.

From the top of your toothbrush-gelled edges,
to the bottom of your strutting toes,

I want everyone to see you.

For your beauty, that persists after centuries
of being chipped away by sharpened blades and watchful
eyes that keep you chained to an image you never owned,

I need you.

To heal my skin that has been left dry from a lifetime

of weathering words, being thrown around by rough-skinned hands
and trapped on an island comprised of weeping souls

Just hold me, Black Woman, and tell me when it's over—
when we have made it to paradise. I hope Her words are true, and that it's nice.

Amari Dawn Pollard is a digital storyteller dedicated to creating space for overlooked narratives within culture, wellness, and sports. She has worked for brands such as Wirecutter, Athletes Unlimited, The Week, and more. She also co-hosts ESPN's "Sound On with Tari & Amari." Amari's creative works have been published in Le Moyne College's *The Salamander* and Folkway Press's *We Are Not Shadows* and have won her three Newhouse Writing Awards. Her other work has been featured in *The Week*, MindBodyGreen, *Bustle*, VeryWell, *Reader's Digest*, *Inside Lacrosse*, and more.

A QUESTION ABOUT HAIR

by Võ Phương Loan

I was talking with a friend.
She, a White woman of a certain age,
We chatted about hair…

My hair has been falling out so much.

I said, "So, I should get a haircut.
But I am not sure what style, what cut…
I don't know what would be flattering anymore.
    Not at all."

"Oh, that reminds me," she said,
"…I must schedule an appointment…
My roots are showing!"

I, too, worry about roots.
But not "my roots are showing."

Vietnamese people say
Tooth and hair are the root of a person.

"For whatever reason, my hair has been falling
so much," I told her.
"Stress. You're stressed," she said.

I think of another conversation.

My daughter had asked to get her hair dyed!?
...and something in me died.

"No, colored!" she corrected.
"why?" I asked.
"It's cool!"
(I felt coldness–in me. Perhaps, from me to
my child. How could this be?)

I have questions. Maybe, too many questions.

What's not okay about the color of your hair?
Is it too black?
Is it too ethnic?

She looked away.
I looked at her.
In my eyes:

There is a haze.
There is a blur.

I, too, worry about the roots.
The roots. Yet small things: strands of hair

Is it too flimsy of a tie?
My daughter and I
Our selves
Our heritage

What is yours and what is mine?
What do we do with this?
…and, still, what do we do with our hair?

Võ Phương Loan is a naturalized citizen who began life in the US as a Vietnamese American refugee and immigrant. She works and teaches as a clinical social worker. She writes to learn and contain her thoughts.

THE MODEL MINORITY

EXPERIENCES LESS RACISM FROM SOCIAL DISTANCING

by Roy Wang

When we were no longer getting together
in spitting range, I didn't hear
any anti-Chinese bullshit
except from the president.
I mean, also dating apps,
but you can't filter nitrogen
out of the air, virtual or real.

The Wuhan flu resurrected
the face of Fu Manchu
I'll keep my mask on a bit longer, thanks.

You can't micro-aggress
when opportunity has egressed
via our high-tech non-essential

window that is closing,
my brethren who still
don't say Black Lives Matter
blind to this perhaps in their race
for round-eyed vantages,
perspective forced
by oxygen-deprived
illusions of meritocracy
to sight only panoramic depths of field.

Inertness, or to use the white devil's
language, passivity,
is a tool, not a state of being;
it gets us what we want
at the predetermined price,
not a safe space to forget
gun-grey evenings
clutching at stems of roses,
pointing out the spade-shaped
cockscomb-red divots in your pork
fists and crying that English
beauty is not for you.

Roy Wang (he/she/they) is a queer, non-binary, polyamorous, Chinese-Canadian poet living in Brooklyn. He has been published in ANMLY, The Windsor Review, Sine Theta, with work forthcoming in CanLit and The Antigonish Review. She was also a finalist in the Two Sylvia's chapbook contest.

LIVING AND BREATHING CHALLENGED

by Christopher D. Sims

You do not think we
should be living, breathing.
You would rather we
not live, breathe
like you do. You live
without any precautions,
or restrictions, or judgements.

You breathe with privilege.
You breathe as if you know
you are going to make it home
safely.

You breathe in front of
the police. You breathe
anywhere, everywhere,
without a care.

You have been given
a right to live, to breathe,
while that same right has
been held from Black people,
brown people. For us, to breathe
is often challenged, tried, lethal.

For us, our chests tighten,
our hearts beating fast,
feeling a choking sensation
in our throats.

Isn't it crazy? We are human.
We are people. You would think
it is unreasonable we would
be questioning our humanity.

This is insanity.

Eric Garner told you he could not
breathe, but you kept going. Police
keep showing the world how they
dare our kind to breathe, dare us
to believe we should take in the
same air; dare us to inhale, exhale,
inhale, exhale, inhale, exhale.

I need oxygen to breathe. Is yours
made of the same kind? Does your
oxygen have the same nutrients?

Is it made of something more
significant? Why should my
living or breathing be any more
different than yours?

White person, is your
breathing copywritten?

Why should mine be
forbidden?

Why is my Black being
caught up in a system
full of so much hate,
violence, division?

You judge my living and breathing
with so much precision; it is a given
I am followed, stopped, harassed, choked,
shot.

I got
two lungs,

two nostrils,
and my gospel
is life.

But, you don't want me
to have life, to breathe.

You simply,
don't want
me to be.

Christopher D. Sims is a poet who challenges this country's treatment of Black people. He has been writing since the age of nine. Christopher has performed all over the United States and in Canada. Currently residing in Rockford, Illinois, he continues to write and perform.

ON MIDWESTERN RURAL LAND

by andrea valeria duarte-alonso

i am housed on the land
that is not of my
ancestors;
my ancestors thrived
on green, luscious,
mountainous, grounds, that give birth
to thick-hanging, ripe aguacate and strong,
standing rows of maiz.

i have been raised by the first
to travel north, paving a new foundation on
land that also offers fields of corn and the constant
stare of the judgmental white human.
generational trauma and assimilation torments
our dreams. yet there is hope, the same one that
helped my parents to walk miles on end, that has planted
seeds filled with love and care.

i stare at my mother's chocolate-almond-shaped
eyes longing for richness, my father's stern face with melted
eyes that continue to hold faith for what can still
become.
i glance down at their cracked, wrinkly hands, and I gently
hold them, wondering if they feel the immense gratitude
through my child-like hands as they continue to hold down
unprecedented, fertile ground.

andrea valeria duarte-alonso is a first-generation, Mexican-American from the great plains of the Midwest. Born in Dodge City, Kansas to immigrant parents working in the meat-processing industry, she had the opportunity to live in multiple small towns that are largely populated with immigrant families. Her experience as a Latina in small towns is a recurring theme in many of her writings. She's a poet, freelance writer, and educator based in Worthington, Minnesota.

CRUSTACEA

by Suzi Mezei

My genealogy is replete with European
        names, nine point Times New Roman,
                proof that under my brown shell
        lurks a thousand white sinews, once prized
in my country, a national saving grace. But I
        don't trust
my history, the faux way it's inscribed, or the way
the lives   of others are omissions or oversights,
kin incised by razor-edits for imperialist
consistency. There's always a story that's alpha,
        imposing, a tyrant narrative
that tears out tongues, a chronicle that's born
with one fist clenched and the other
        filching whatever it can get,
        official versions   with obdurate vocal cords
                                that shout-down objections
and intentionally oppress. My genealogy, is replete
with European names,   my brown hand

can trace the great great's Belgian place of birth,
the Zeeland harbor where Jacobus   stepped
on a gangway that led to   a new world.
My family's old world is cluttered with Dutch Reform
and Catholic mass, whalebone corsets and colonial
constructions, mired in allegiance to restricted clubs
that only recently   died from shame.
      Absent are the native names,
dark as jungles, the ones that make western tongues
curl, contort;   absent are the tethered gods
of voiceless ancestors, of those deemed unworthy
of dialogue;
                                                        they are lost.
I shiver in the gaps that history   left unfilled. A chill
flows through those holes;
dark   gouges like the burrows left
by mangrove crabs   in unsettled silt.

Suzi Mezei is a Sri Lankan-born Australian writer. She lives in Naarm on land traditionally owned by the Boonwurrung people. Suzi's work is influenced by her culture and experience. The work appears in Australia and overseas in journals and anthologies including *Best of Australian Poems*, *Burrow*, *Aniko*, *Cordite* and *Hecate*. She has received an artist's residency.

WE ARE COUNTRIES MADE OF CLAY

INSPIRED BY MAHOGANY L. BROWN "COUNTRY OF WATER"

by Fairouz Bsharat

When you were finding yourself, did you first have to sink before finding your way to the surface? Sometimes I search for words in the hyphen between Palestinian-American. Then the black ink becomes the last color on "my" flag. Green, white, black, with a red triangle. The red comes from a little boy shot in his own home. His blood seeps its way onto the flag. With every wave, we mourn him.

I mourn the pieces of myself I lost to a blue-eyed blonde named "Beauty." She chases me everywhere, and like every monster, she's particularly fond of the night. When you look in a mirror, did you wish your nose was smaller? Sometimes I wish mine was up-turned but not turned up at others. Were you sad when your arms were grabbed, put next to Beauty, and you were told you weren't "light enough" to be pretty and not "dark enough" to fit in with the outcasts?

My tears aren't clear, that means that every Disney princess collects them in jars and forces me to drink them for every sit-up done in the dead of night. My body is an hourglass that counts down to an unknown time. If I wrap the words tight enough around my waist, will I finally be skinny enough to walk between books pressed against each other and stacked on a shelf?

Did you repeat "I know" so many times to affirm to others who you are, or convince yourself that you know? Your heart beats blood in timed measures, but music isn't just the metronome. If I take two eighth notes, flip them, and beat my head like a drum, is that music? My cries in the night are silent. Can silence be music?

If the quiet isn't heard by anyone, except the stars, is it still unheard of? The moon hears them, thinks, and spits them back at me in terror. Women hide behind anything they can to align themselves with society. The moon hides behind the sun. Is a solar eclipse really a phenomenon or just the stars telling us to search for help in the heavens?

If I take a sip of water after reading your poem, will the paper fold itself into a boat? Will the ink become a crew and the spaces between the oars? Is the crew's skin darkened from the sun? I think they too are trapped in the trance of colored eyes and forgetting that brown is the color of life. From the dirt we were created and to the dirt we will return. Our skin isn't dirt-colored, just sun kissed and hugged by tree bark. Our skin is life-colored.

Fairouz Bsharat is a junior Literary Arts major at Appomattox Regional Governor's School for the Arts and Technology and the current Virginia Youth Poet Laureate for Chester! She has won first place in the Fledge National Fiction Competition, been named a young poet in the community by the poetry society of VA, and has had her poetry published in Appelley Publishing Magazine, Young Writers USA, Virginia Bards

Central Review 2022, American High School Poets - May Flowers 2023 Anthology, and in ASGARD (our own school literary magazine). She has also seen first-hand how poetry affects the lives of people everywhere. Poetry helps people express themselves! Expression is the best way to avoid conflict. If one has words to cradle them, often their solace is always sought.

REMEMBER ROSE*

SYRIA, AFGHANISTAN

by Marieke Slovin Lewis

(Arabic)

ديهشلا انأ ةديهشلا انأ

'ana alshahidat 'ana alshahid

ديهشلا انأ

'ana alshahid

انا

'ana

Remember Rose, she's nine years old
She never lived to tell you this
Remember Rose, she's nine years old
Killed by the bombs in Saraqib

(Arabic)

ديهشلا انأ ةديهشلا انأ

'ana alshahidat 'ana alshahid

ديهشلا انأ
'ana alshahid
انا
'ana

Come back, come back, everything you are
Muslim, Christian, whatever you are
If you broke your promise one hundred times
Come back, I will be here

(Arabic)
ديهشلا انأ   ةديهشلا انأ
'ana alshahidat 'ana alshahid
ديهشلا انأ
'ana alshahid
انا
'ana

(Dari)
درگربدرگرب
Bazay, bazay, come back, come back
درگربدرگرب
Bazay, bazay, come back, come back
درگربدرگرب
Bazay, bazay, come back, come back

(Arabic)
انا
'ana

Marieke Slovin Lewis is a participatory artist, musician, and writer. She composes music using a method of songwriting called Story-to-Song (STS), which she co-created as a doctoral student studying Sustainability Education. Through STS, Marieke guides a person through the creative process of shaping a personal story into a song.

---

* "Remember Rose" is a song Marieke composed with Scottish poet and writer Sarah Reader Harris and refugees from Syria and Afghanistan while they were in residence at the Fedasil Arrival Centre in Brussels, awaiting a response to their applications for asylum in Belgium. Rose was a nine year old girl who was a friend to the Syrian refugee. She was killed by bombing in Saraqib. "Shaheeda" means witness in Arabic and can also mean martyr. The words "Baza, Baza" at the end of the song were shared by a young man from Afghanistan. They mean "Come back" in Dari. "Remember Rose" is one of dozens of songs guided into being during poetry and songwriting sessions Marieke and Sarah offered on Mondays at the Fedasil Arrival Centre from January 2017 to March 2020. This creative work, which they called the "Migration Songs Project," was a finalist for the Amateo Award for arts participation projects in Europe in 2021.

DON'T SAY GAY

by Jennifer Elise Wang

When I was eleven, my mother told me to stop saying "gay"
Because a synonym for "weird" or "uncool" was not "gay."

When I was fourteen, MTV taught me about Matthew
Shepard:
That you could be not just jeered but also killed for being gay.

Now DeSantis and his ilk don't want kids to learn about
Stonewall
Or read books geared toward them with a character who's
gay.

We're not supposed to don our gay apparel outside of
Christmas;
Those with a beard can't feel pretty, witty, and gay.

They can try to tell us to "Don't Say Gay" especially in
front of kids,

But even if the word has disappeared, we will be
here and gay.

We'll just say homosexual, lesbian, bi, pan, trans-
gender, non-binary—
I am a genderqueer ace, but to defy them, I'll call
myself "gay."

Jennifer Elise Wang (she/they) is a neurodivergent non-binary femme in STEM and punk rock pretty boi poet from Dallas, Texas. When she's in lab or writing, she enjoys cosplaying, dancing, and learning how to skateboard and snowboard. They have been published in *The New Verse News*, *just femme & dandy*, *Vocivia*, and *Ofic*.

WHO KILLED DAVEY MOORE?

by Nnadi Samuel

"Not me, says the boxing writer. Sayin', Boxing ain't to blame,
There's just as much danger in a football game. Sayin',
Fist fighting is here to stay. It's just the old American way."—Bob Dylan

"Don't come back, they'll kill you for being gay."— BBC NEWS

at the sleight of my arm, each eyelid folds in bloodshot grace.
my fury, breaking jaws in disgraced light—that sends the world
crumbling. the rough collision, met by an ovoid-mobbed face.

a gay slur to my ear is a call to glove, the way I unspeak my rage
in dreadful thunder blows. we all started out as a blunder.
one more misgendering & the gingiva fits well for a punching bag.

you should beware of what precedes my fist:

I waltz in the showmanship of a deranged coyote—aiming for the jowl,
when I throw caution to the wind, kneading your flesh to its elastic point.

I wear the sad properties of Hooke's law. the grieving lies in the aftermath
of a punch: this ceremonious un-aliving of my gender.
think of this murder as what leaves me few months shy of my grave.

I swear to you, loving a boy around here would do much worse.
I debone the cheek, rupture his ribcage in one deathblow
& stay gorgeous—dressing the breath to one brief sigh.

the unspoken rule of boxing states that: "*A welter-weight fighter remain*
answerable to an opponent-turn-ghost." where do I draw the line between
mercy & *mercy killing*, if not in the way blood guts the alphabet?

a dent to the loamy soft skin. the aching red, breeding from within:
a banquet of hurt. a thoughtful felony. I slacken my fist to rid off

the mashed ligament sticking bone-close to joint, & they
tighten back.

when I approach a boy, gender bear stains.

Nnadi Samuel (he/him/his) holds a B.A in English & literature from the University of Benin. Author of *'Nature knows a little about Slave Trade'* selected by Tate.N.Oquendo (Sundress Publication, 2023). A 3x Best of the Net, and 7x Pushcart Nominee. He won the *2022 Angela C Mankiewicz Poetry Contest and Bronze prize for the Creative Future Writer›s Award 2022, UK London.*

INTERVIEW WITH MEMPHIS' BELLA DUBALLE,

DRAG QUEEN/MINISTER, AS CHURCH BELLS PLAY ALL THINGS BRIGHT AND BEAUTIFUL (WITH WORDS FROM NPR'S FRESH AIR, MARCH 18, 2023)

by S.E.B. Detling

"When a straight person [dresses in drag],
it's a joke. 'I put on this dress because it is to take
on femininity, which is less than my masculinity.
So, don't we laugh at that? Look at how sissified I am.'"

All things bright and beautiful
All creatures great and small
All things wise and wonderful
The Lord God made them all

"When I [Bella DuBalle] put on a dress
it is a statement of strength. It is a statement
of how powerful my femininity is. So, for me, I think
it's about the way we approach the feminine."

Each little flower that opens
Each little bird that sings
God made their glowing colors
God made their tiny wings

"The patriarchy has always used drag
as another way to reinforce that women are weaker.
I think we as the queer community
actually champion that pride, that femininity."

The purple-headed mountains
The rivers running by
The sunset and the morning
That brightens up the sky

"These legislations are aimed at trying to diminish
or erase us. Trying to get us to sit down and be quiet.
I think the response to that is to be louder
and more in your face, be bolder. Let them
understand…"

The cold wind in the winter
The pleasant summer sun
The ripe fruits in the garden
God made them, every one

"...we are not a threat to society, we are a part of it.
We belong here too. [...] I have received threats of violence
and death threats and such. I have been confronting bullies
since I was 5 years old, so this is nothing new to me."

God gave us eyes to see them
And lips that we might tell
How great is the Almighty
Who has made all things well

S.E.B. Detling is a poet, instructor, editor, and mother in Mobile, AL. She won the Alabama State Poetry Society's Fall 2021 Contest and was a finalist in the Poetry by Moonlight 2022 Contest. Her poetry has appeared in *The Pinch*, *The Dead Mule*, *Poetry South*, *Birmingham Arts Review*, *Negative Capability*, and others.

FIRST MIRROR SELFIE

WITHOUT THE PRESENCE OF PINK FLOWERS

by Hassan Usman

"Lawmaker Seeks Six Months Jail Term, N500,000 Fine for Crossdressers in Nigeria"— Channels Television, 5th April 2022

What unrolls its beauty into cages?
I mean to say, I'd miss this frequent travel into

wholesomeness—how I'd garb myself with my mother's
Iro and Buba, as she does, and watch this drama grow
    into a habit.

Here, you are meant to be conventional, fully Muslim, and
never ungovernable. Today, instead of frolicking around
    this city in

my sister's leg chains, I sneak into the calligraphy of a rock.
Liberalism no be for Africans. Which means,

I have to be less white, more Nigerian black. Brother,
if you return home a crossdresser, your body would become

an item that shouldn't be kept away from burning.
This is how I live now—turning my body inside out to
find joy.

I am born in a country where boys cannot be delighted by
the painting of their nails, the braiding of their hairs.

Once, my father called me a scarecrow, a wannabe princess.
But today, I am the god of war, straight as a square.

I deleted all my Instagram posts resembling the Venus
symbol.
No boy suppose dey dress or waka like woman. Hence I head
home.

I burn the makeup kit that has been smearing my life
with infamy.
I don't know what bliss this transition will bring, but

to live, knowing your mother could call you her
husband, is
as much a form of survival as necessary.

Hassan A. Usman, NGP II, is a Black poet and a lover of cats. His works have appeared or forthcoming in *Blue Route Journal*, *Baltimore Review*, *Invisible Lit*, *The Madrigal Press*, *Paper Lanterns*, *Trampset*, *Icefloe Press*, *Poetrycolumn-NND*, *Nymph*, *SprinNG*, *Kissing Dynamite Poetry*, *The Shallow Tales Review*, *Olumo Review*, *Arts Lounge*, *Five South*, and elsewhere. He's an alumnus of the SprinNG Writing Fellowship 2022. Hassan enjoys cooking, listening to Nigerian street music, and juggles writing with modelling. Say hi to him on Twitter or Instagram @Billio_Speaks.

DON'T SMILE AT MEN

by Amanda Hiland

Men are afraid that women will laugh at them. Women are afraid that men will kill them.— Margaret Atwood

My mother told me:

Don't smile at men
when you're out alone.
If you do, they might think
you're opening yourself to them.
They might try to talk to you,
and of course you'll talk back
(you don't want to be rude, a bitch, a cunt),
and then there goes your afternoon.
If you smile at him, he might want more,
and if you don't give it, he might sneer and say,
Why did you smile if you don't want attention?
I bet you walk around,
giving smiles to all the men, whoring out your lips
and teeth and tongue.

Practice keeping your face a blank façade,
a true neutral. Don't look back when he looks at you.
Focus on a detail of the room, something over his shoulder—
a sign, a painting, the carved relief of a table.
Study it
as if you can see its history,
as if you're going to write a poem about it.
If you need to, you can close your eyes,
pretend you're thinking deeply
until your proximity sensors stop thrumming.
Make your body a concave figure,
ceding space as you retreat inward.

Maybe that sounds hard, a life spent fading
into the background,
but I promise it gets easier
the more you practice. And if you do it right,
you may live long enough
to feel the sunlight of your own
daughter's smile and to know the terror
that compels you to smother it.

Amanda Hiland is a queer writer who grew up hiking through the forests of Oregon. A Special Education teacher by day, she is also a major astronomy enthusiast at night. She spends her free time folding origami, traveling, and advocating for underserved communities. Her work has appeared most recently in *VoiceCatcher*, *Epiphany*, *Willawaw Journal*, and *Cathexis*.

THIS IS NOT A POLITICAL POEM

by Tay Stafford

Am I
somewhere between these rectangular dimensions—
I mean, page. I must imprint proof of aspiration
onto each faded blue line which tempts to crowd
me like a herded sheep. You ought
to know that my essence supersedes
clauses and tenses. This is a voyage through
the page before the words summon existence
through the physical plane where the wood
panels of universities structures blindfold
where thou and I meet I've ignored
the Mother of days creation like a tree
trunk reaching miles beneath itself her
undressed branches whose edges could free
bloom through this black body
I am anything besides what you call me—
Yes.

I am majestic, inoculated
by the colonizer's language, perpetually I
utilize their function like wet
sand trying to escape itself
My truth has been connived by ghostly faces to
terrify me
They say I am a tempestuous beast
left hopelessly free falling into
photosynthesized leaves that crouch near a dead
sequoia—the agony slips out the
sclera brailing dew onto my body
No. I am a gold beam
of light plated with dazzling rain drops—the
dew dribbles into pianos and guitar strings that snap,
pops slithering through wiggling my ancestors bodies
I am Theolonus Monk
I am B.B King

—I recline like a stretched palm
underneath dismal clouds with suggestions from gray
infused with sun light that stretches————
at length I am the suns
honeyed rum that revivifies
my psyche I am my tongue.

Tay Stafford identifies as a teacher, writer, and entrepreneur. Tay graduated with a master's in fine arts from Western Washington University (2023). Through the art of writing, Tay healed childhood trauma, and quickly gathered an understanding of how trauma can develop and rot in the body if not released with grace, acceptance, compassion, and love. Tay's poems traverse complex subjects such as (but not limited to) transgenerational trauma, identity, the impermanence of relationships, and spirituality. Tay poems have been published in, *Between Fact & Fiction: A Whatcom Writes Anthology*; Whatcom READS and Village Books, *At This Juncture*; and Western Washington University Art Gallery. *Right to Life* from Folkway Press will be Tay's third publication. Tay partners with a non-profit organization, RIS3 Athletic Academy (established in 2019), and teaches English at Highline College in the state of Washington. Tay can be found on Instagram, @ris3ambassador, and Facebook as well.

SWING STATE

By Anastasia Jill

I learned to walk inside this
body— lay my bones in elephant
skin, ugly, chubby,
a weak pundit
to shame the wise.

But the wise do not make
progress; they do not shake the
world.
I live in a world of blue—
breathless blue, single-payer blue,
good old American blue-collar
blue,   deoxygenated and
universal blue, but still blue no
matter who

smears my coquettish smile,
finds the pit-bull beneath the lipstick.

The big daddy dog is me;
wearing freedom like a dress
that makes dirty men speak in half-
terms. And with certainty, I love these
men.
But I am no Sarah Palin

because this body is not a state
but two arms with weak wrists,
with both hands swearing
they're the good guy with the gun.

Left hand, right hand.
It doesn't matter who pulls the trigger,
My ugly body will be left red—
collateral red, partisan red,
rejected, red slip,
crack and whipped up
red,   the red left on
read,
but in the end,
unpicked yet scabby,
red.

Anastasia Jill (they/them) is a queer, neuro-divergent writer living in Central Florida. They have been nominated for Best American Short

Stories, The Pushcart Prize, and several other honors. Their work has been featured or is upcoming with Poets.org, *Sundog Lit*, *Flash Fiction Online*, *Contemporary Verse 2*, *Broken Pencil*, and more.

FOLD YOUR TEARS INTO PEACE SIGNS

by Dianna MacKinnon Henning

When your neighbor is the enemy
and Night pulls its sharpened knife,

a word does what a word must.
It summons its bloodhounds.

Wheat fields turn barren.
An old woman pours seeds

into a soldier's jacket pocket.
When he's later shot down,

sunflowers will blossom his gravesite.
(Beauty's reprieve in all the mayhem.)

Sooty debris smudges the streets.
Neither the notations of loss, nor

the uncompromising hand of indifference
assuages the survivors. War's a thug who sucks

his thumb in a limousine's backseat
and gorges on caviar.

Diana MacKinnon Henning received a MFA in Writing Vermont College in 1989. Her fourth poetry book, "Camaraderie of the Marvelous," was published by Kelsay Books in 2021. She is a six-time Pushcart Nominee. Dianna taught through California Poets in the Schools, received several California Arts Council grants and taught poetry workshops through the William James Association's Prison Arts Program. She runs The Thompson Peak Writers' Workshop in Lassen County. Publications, in part: *Poet News*, Sacramento; *Worth More Standing, Poets and Activists Pay Homage to Trees*; *Voices*; *MacQueen's Quinterly*; *Artemis Journal*, 2021 & 2022; *The Adirondack Review; Memoir Magazine* and *New American Writing.*

EPITAPH FOR THE LIVING

by Ona Wang

What indulgence
to have hobbies   instead of battles

What reverence
for names to be a mouthful
not bite-size chunks   gummed gristle

What satisfaction
to chew "what if"   without bitter aftertaste

What liberation
to be bold   in moonlight
not shrink from slinking indigo shadows

What license
to know a body as a fortress   not forfeit   or barter

What simplicity
to be more   than a name
to settle into draping arms   grow into your sagging belly
smile stretched across   the constellation of your teeth

What immunity
To meet fear the moment your heart stops
and not its reverse   to find respite only in rest

What ease
to grow old   then forgetful
instead of remembered as potential

What contentment
to deteriorate
watch the next generation outpace you
outgrow you
students teach you   instead of saying your name

What luxury
to be wrong   instead of dead

What freedom
to ask yourself how you want to be remembered
instead of becoming an activist in death
instead of becoming a martyr with your last breath

What joy
to be remembered for what you say in life
instead of
your last words

Ona Wang is a social practice artist, educator, researcher, and restorative justice practitioner from Chicago. Committed to addressing complex and community trauma through restorative justice and creative practice, Ona applies storytelling as a tool for community building, solidarity, and healing. Ona holds a background in peacebuilding, behavioral science, and civic engagement.

PROSE

THE DIARY OF A YOUNG GIRL

by Lauren Meir

[Writer's note: Some of the italicized phrases in this piece were taken from The Diary of Anne Frank.]

I

Dear Kitty,

It began the way it always begins: An open book
the pages blank, a gift. How we thrill at the possibility,
Anne Frank and I, twins separated by five decades
confessing our newly teenage dramas.

Only I am still here. Unhidden, alive.

She spent 761 days in the attic,
quietly scratching away at the shifting

voices, the fears jutting up, her dreams
swelling like a prayer over her narrow shoulders.

I think of my grandmother: her name is Olga.
Imprisoned in the same concentration camps
at the same time: Auschwitz and Bergen-Belsen.
Sinister on the tongue, their names
an infection that won't die.

II

Dear Kitty,

Can I tell you a secret?

I play a game, where I pretend
Anne and Olga
become friends. Dark-eyed and nameless,
they find each other somehow
in the gray sea of broken
women. They could almost be sisters.
It's an impossibility that exists
somewhere in the realm of possible.

Olga Jakabovitz is 25, a decade older
than Annalise Frank. But both love books;
both adore their fathers; both are tethered

by dreams too heavy for this place, still cradling
the frail hope that *people are really good at heart.*

Even here, even now.

They have no common language. They are from different
countries. But what does that matter, in this endless death
factory? *You don't think of all the misery but of the beauty
that still remains.* You remember:
You are still human.
You hold onto this.
You don't let go.

III

Dear Kitty,

This is how it goes:

At night in the barracks,
Olga tells Anne stories of make believe. They huddle
together for warmth and memory, imagining
themselves children in some dystopian Hansel
and Gretel nightmare that they can survive
if they push the Nazis into their own ovens.

They almost laugh at the absurd accuracy
And then they do—soundlessly, hands-over-mouths,
gasping, their frail bodies aching from effort.
Unsure if it's joy or grief or something else,
eyes closed to blot out the dead rolling up
in great waves of smoke.

IV

Dear Kitty,

In Bergen-Belsen it is February, and bitterly cold.
The girls are so thirsty they want to drink sewage.
If only they knew the British were on their way,
the Russians closing in—soon they will be liberated.

It is fifty years later, and I am 13,
holding onto this truth, willing Anne to know it—
to survive.

The whole world is waiting, and many are waiting
for death, she writes. I want to erase it,
as though she won't die inside
the black letters of her own words.

Anne. Annalise. Annaleh,
Olga calls softly,

her name, their names, any name
an act of defiance, a refusal
to be some forgettable number.
Erased.

Just hold on, Olga whispers in every language she knows:
Hungarian. Romanian. Yiddish. German. English.
Don't let go.

V

Dear Kitty,

It is 1995, and I've sung my haftorah.
I am chosen, exulted; it is my bat-mitzvah.
I wear a black-and-white dress. I know that I am beautiful.
I know that I am a woman with inward strength and plenty of courage.
Someone lets me sip champagne. I dance shoeless,
until I can no longer feel my swollen feet.
Everything glows.

My grandmother watches me from a solitary corner,
alone at the table, her food untouched. Still she smiles,
an extraordinary thing, like the moon in daylight.
I watch as light swells around her in an embrace, like wings
closing over and over. The numbers on her forearm
bleed into one another with age.

Never again.
And again
and again and again.

VI

Dear Kitty,

I am 25 and living in Europe, my boots hollow
on the silent cobblestone streets of a Jewish Quarter
empty of Jews. I hear it chanted like an incantation,
like the mournful sounds of davening, an echo of a question:
Live or Die, Live or Die…

It floats above my dark hair like a crown. As though
there are only two options. I know it before I hear it.
A voice breaking a silent window in protest:

Just hold on.

I stand at the edge of Charles Bridge,
considering the Vltava River. It is black and cold
and ancient. Lovers leave locks hooked to its sides,
an act of devotion. A promise.

I had to find a reason, my grandmother tells me.
I had to find something to live for.
I walk away from the bridge alone. O, shooting star....

I am hoping I will be able to confide in you
as I have never been able to confide in anyone.

Lauren Meir is a writer and communications professional working in philanthropy. She has lived in both Europe and the Middle East, writing her way through countries and cultures. Her work has appeared in the *Huffington Post*, the *Detroit Jewish News*, *Voidspace*, the *Amethyst Review* and *Musing Publications,* among others. She lives with her family in metro Detroit. Find her on twitter at @LaurenMeir or see more of her work at LaurenMeir.com.

CITIZEN OF NOWHERE

by Daisy Rossignol

I don't remember my father's homeland.

Sometimes I think I do—a sunset, a snatch of song, or the gingery spice of someone's perfume at the market. But I was barely walking when we left, stubby legs swaddled into a basket on my mother's back to leave her hands free, and by that point, there were no sunsets. No expensive scents. If a pink sky makes me think of the old world, it's a memory of burning books and temples, the flames so high they turned the clouds red and the raindrops hissed and steamed before they hit the ground.

Little candle, my father used to call me. He had loved my red hair.

But when you've seen fire devour your home, when you've had to run with your children and the clothes on your back and leave everything and everyone you love behind, it's hard to go back to thinking of a candle as a source of light.

Once, I tried to talk to my brother about it. He was five years older than me, and I thought he'd understand the confused memories better than I did. The sense of belonging to both worlds and to neither. Of trying to cling on to a whole universe, now reduced to a tattered old shawl and snatches of a language neither of us could remember how to speak. But he poured himself a mug of coffee—coffee, not the tea our parents drank—and disappeared with his bag slung low over his back like his friends.

My brother had learnt to hide himself, by then. To turn himself into a dark-eyed baseball pitcher, charming and funny. A human chameleon.

I suppose I did the same. I had the right accent. I rode the bus. I watched the programmes the popular kids at school watched so that I could join in the conversations at lunch.

But when I ducked through the curtain over the door to our apartment, it felt like a mask came off. There was my father, the sleeves of his tunic rolled up and his glasses almost opaque with steam as he bent over the stove, three pans bubbling away. There was my mother at her loom, shuttle flashing backwards and forwards as she wove golden-threaded carpets. And I didn't need to hold it in anymore, either. I could leave my homework at the door and stop making myself small to fit in.

Aria, my mother would say without turning her head.

I'd step close and place a hand on her shoulder, and the magic she wove into her tapestries jolted like electricity. She taught me to close my eyes, to concentrate on that thread and to join my own magic to it. And as I became stronger, I started to feel the other survivors sending their power through the strands and adding their spells to my mother's workings. The other witches who still believed in the old world and who gathered night after night to send help back to those who still cried out for aid. Together, we wove intricate patterns, and in the threads, we reinforced bridges and ran supports under collapsed homes until survivors could be pulled from the rubble. We probed the enemy's defences, looking for weaknesses, and we told stories of good luck and victory in the pictures woven by the loom. And every night we'd finish exhausted, a happy burn in our limbs, and we'd sell the carpets to tourists to send the magic out into the world, and neither my mother nor my father would admit what we all knew. That there weren't enough of us left anymore to win this war.

The fields of my father's homeland were littered with corpses, and there hadn't been time to bury them.

The cities of my father's homeland had been reduced to rubble picked over by black-clad men, and there weren't enough of us to rebuild them.

The language of my father's homeland, the magic of my father's homeland, was dying by inches, and there weren't enough of us left to keep the dream alive.

My mother had always hoped that my brother and I would join the fight together, and when he went to college instead, it broke her heart. He came home at Christmas, scuffed his heels and looked mulish that we didn't celebrate, and when the spring festival came and we climbed onto our building's roof to lie in the moonlight and tell the stories written in the stars, he stayed away.

Eventually, he stopped coming back at all.

I thought I missed him, but really, I was missing the idea of him. The brother I hoped he'd be, who would tell me the stories of our childhood and fill the gap between the world we lived in and the world we'd left. But that brother had never existed, so I swallowed the stone in my throat. I learnt my mother's songs and wove them into carpets that thrummed with magic, the shuttle flashing red and gold, telling the stories we had loved before the war. I cooked with my father, guessing at the ingredients when he couldn't remember the recipe his grandfather had taught him. Our home was full of laughter and the taste of my childhood, but at school, people wrinkled their noses and shifted away from the smell caught in my hair.

Come out dancing, they said sometimes. *You belong here now.*

But sometimes they'd laugh behind their hands, twist gum into my braids or make jokes about bombs and knives. And I would ball my hands into fists so tight that my nails left half-moon bruises in my palms, and bite my tongue until it bled, as though that would prove to them that my father and my family and my people were not the savages they wanted us to be.

My mother's soul passed into the next world, and my father and I drove her body out to the high mountains and buried her under the moon and the stars. I felt numb, eyes dry, until I tied gold coins around my wrists and hot tears fell at last, ripped from somewhere deep inside me that had broken long ago, when the temples burned. The last witch, taking over the mantle from my mother, grandmother, great-grandmother, as far back as the stories could go. My father cut his beard, and when he whispered the prayer for the living and the dead over my mother's shrouded body, I heard him utter my brother's name, too.

So there were two of us.

And I lived in this world, the world of contactless credit cards and queuing on the freeway to spend ten hours earning less than minimum wage and then picking over the reduced section on the way home. And I lived in the shadow world, of blinding desert heat and camps full of women and children who had been stolen from their homes and sold, of haggling over carpets, of substituting the flavours in my father's cooking for the closest equivalent we could find at the store, and of the electric thrum of magic that we had to clutch tightly to our chests lest it break free from our calloused fingertips and remind the world that we were here.

All of this for a country that no longer existed.

That never would again.

A country I couldn't even remember.

There were anniversary articles in newspapers and long analytical reports funded by thinktanks. Strangers marched in the capital carrying placards, and strangers debated the term *genocide*.

It was a world away from the songs, the prayers, the smell of ginger and the jangle of anklets in the moonlight.

The clinical speeches and the tweets about war crimes came from people who had never seen the sunrise over the mountains, had never eaten fresh bread and honey and argued about whose turn it was to read the tealeaves.

But I couldn't explain that to them, because I hadn't done those things either. I just knew that they had mattered, once. An echo on the breeze.

The community shrank. Some moved, their names joining my brother's in the long prayer for the living and the dead, and some just moved on. Every year, the strands of magic arcing around those of us who were left became weaker. The stories of survival coming out of the old world became rarer, and sadder, until my heart ached. I sat at my mother's loom, but the threads tangled in my fingers, and there was no answering thrum of prayer and power to smooth the pattern and turn our dreams into something real.

When my father's soul moved on, it felt like all the candles in the sky had blown out at once.

I floated, for a while.

Lost the apartment and moved into my car.

Lost one job.

Lost another.

But spring came, and moonlight, and the old songs on the breeze.

I threaded gold coins into my hair. Traded my jeans for red and gold thread to mend my father's tunics and my mother's skirts. Learnt to cook over a gas hob, set up my mother's loom in the parking lot and pretended I wasn't alone.

A teacher waved me over in the park and invited me into school for Culture Day. I swallowed down the bitterness in my heart and went, wishing all the time that I had stayed away.

Afterwards, a journalist came.

A radio station.

Then a text from an unknown number. *I think your mother knew my mother.* The tiniest thread of light.

A debate on morning television. *They're economic migrants. They should go back to where they came from.* I caught the tail end of the show through a shop window and watched the two guests they had invited debate my right to exist. Discuss dropping bombs on my father's homeland. Weigh up whether they should have intervened in a civil war. *It wasn't a civil war*, the host said. *This was an invasion. It crossed a border.* The guests looked puzzled, then recovered. *Borders in that part of the world. So confusing. It's all tribal over there. There's not much difference between them.*

A reunion in the capital. A charity paid for me to attend and bought my carpets at a discount to display on the walls. They brought in cameras and politicians, and a makeup artist drew patterns on my cheeks that stayed even after I scrubbed. I didn't recognise myself in the photographs afterwards. *Traditional tribal tattoos*, a journalist explained. But it wasn't true, and they hadn't asked, and I didn't look like me.

An invitation to an award ceremony.

An invitation to shake hands with a politician.

Every time the photographs and the articles, the tutorials online trying to replicate the braids in my hair, the mangled attempts at the food my father and I used to make. Every time the debates. And all the time the feeling of being stretched, longer and thinner and further out of shape, until I began to tear in the middle. All the time questions and responsibility and a dying heritage that was only half mine, because I didn't remember the temples burning and I certainly didn't remember the time before.

Until one day, the last little flame of magic burning in my chest guttered and went out.

A hint of smoke on the breeze.

I stripped the gold coins out of my hair, wiped the kohl from my eyes. I folded away the tunics and skirts, wrapped the shuttle and loom in the last threads of my mother's scarf.

People frowned at my jeans and baggy sweat-shirts. Someone sent me a twitter thread about *cultural abandonment*. But a hot dog and a baseball cap was as much my culture as sitar music and bread dipped in spiced oil. The tv programmes of the country I had grown up in were just as much mine as the stories my father had whispered to my mother under the stars. I had as much and as little claim to both sides of my life.

The journalists didn't understand, and neither did the teachers, nor the politicians.

But when a little girl stepped off a plane clutching a sunflower, and when she called for her father in a language she would soon forget, I saw her. I saw the tired confusion, the pride in her homeland warring with the desire to forget, to fit in, to avoid the whispers and the stares.

I recognised her.

And I said welcome, my sister, for you will belong to everywhere and to nowhere, and you will keep the spirit of your people alive.

I am here to show you how.

YOU PEOPLE

by Emilce Ferreira

Had I been born sooner, I would have been stamped a witch and burned at the stake. Yet, the certainty of that realization does not churn my seas like it used to. The voices of my ancestors warble through generations and borders to whisper in my ear, but time shreds them past recognition. It has become the longest game of telephone ever played.

"Where have you been?" The substitute teacher asked me when my restroom break was longer than she would have liked.

"The restroom, Ms." I smiled.

"Sure, and I'm stupid, right?" Her words were like an ax being sharpened.

"I was," I tried to explain.

"Right. Just sit down. I have a lot of test scores to get through." She abused the papers on her desk to prove it to me. "Others might believe you people, but we both know you are all liars and manipulators. God only knows where you were." Her words hit their mark. She swung at me with her ax and hit my chest with a thud, embedding it in my heart. I shrank into my chair, ashamed at her words. The accusation did not belong to me, but it felt personal. I bent over my desk, wishing the floor would open and swallow me whole. But it wouldn't. At the sound of the period bell, the class filed out under her gaze.

"Catalina, you got commended on your state exam," she hurled at my back as if to dig out the blade. I did not turn back. Instead, I walked out into the seventh-grade halls, never to feel safe in that classroom again. The rest of the day, I sat, trying to suppress the shame and tears when her words escaped the darkness of my mind and tried to take center stage. I had always eluded the torments of my peers by learning to be a phantom, but this teacher had seen me and tried to cast me out like an exorcist. I was a terrible taste in her mouth, and I couldn't understand why. I felt smaller than a worm in the ground. Who was "you people"?

"But I didn't lie," I whispered to my knees when sleep wouldn't come. The accusatory voice of the teacher seemed to be emboldened in the darkness of the night. It berated me when there was nothing I could use to anchor myself and push back on the memory.

It took me a week to realize who "you people" were. After all, she had not been a substitute in the traditional sense but a member of the administration who was forced to dress up as one when they had come up with a teacher too short. Her skin was not as dark as mine, if at all. It quickly became apparent that the arrogance she wielded did not merely come from her title of administrator but something I had never seen before in my mother or any other Mexican woman. Her attitude was one of superiority and pollution.

The wound left behind by her intentionally sharp words followed me for the rest of the school year. The fire I had felt for mathematics was snuffed out while she continued on with her life, oblivious to the damage she had caused. It became obvious that the wreckage she left behind was worth less than if I had come from the suburbs instead of the river.

As the years passed, I carefully applied balm to the weeping wound. Finally, just like the rest, this injury scarred over. But late at night, when the air is still, and the creatures are all sleeping, my chest feels a ghostly ache. The teacher's words echo through the halls of my mind, reaching for me with ghastly fingers. Little do they know I have learned to wield magic and vanish hate, for I did not cross the border to be vanquished by words. So, when the insults rise from their grave, clamoring for blood, I face them head-on and remind them that I am not my ancestors.

Emilce Ferreira is a Mexican-American aspiring writer. She is currently a candidate in the Master of Liberal Arts program at Harvard's Extension School. Emilce likes to spend time with her children and mini-donkeys when not in class or writing.

IMAGE CAPTURE

OR

DEAR FAMILY SHARING BREAKFAST AT IHOP

by Allison Baldwin

It's been many years since I first learned about insiders and outsiders, about what we are, and what we aren't, allowed to tell. And, for the most part, I agree with it.

I know your story isn't mine to tell, yet I imagine that, you too, know something about being an outsider.And, since we were both in the moment I am about to recount, I'll presume that I have my own responsibility in the sharing.

I wish I had captured your faces. At the breakfast table, in the middle of the IHOP, strewn with plates and knives, half-eaten pancake stacks, and over-buttered toast, bitten twice. The whole place smelling of citrus and burnt coffee. You were a large family, seven, if I recall. My best friend and I, who had occupied the table next to yours, were just finishing up and preparing to leave.

I wish I had captured your faces watching her pull my four-wheeled walker over to the booth. I wish I had captured your faces watching me shimmy and shake, push and pull, out of that tight space. I wish I had captured your faces watching me use my arm and back muscles to pull myself up, the compensation for weak legs.

What I remember is, the forgotten plates and knives. What I remember is, your open mouths. What I remember is, how quiet everything got. I've never been stared at so intensely. Outside, my friend said the whole moment was an event for you. We laughed.

***

Years later, I learned about the history of freakshows. Did you know that the circus started because a man named P.T. Barnum wanted to capitalize on distorted bodies? He thought we would be easy money, fifty cents a view. And not just bodies that look like mine but also ones that look like yours. Consumers, lined up along the cobblestones, stared open mouthed. Even paid extra for "private" shows. That was the only time "those types" were allowed in the street.

No, really. There was a law. An ugly law, to be precise. The law was on the books for about twenty years and deemed it illegal for any person considered ugly to expose himself or herself to public view. The one exception was demonstrations because they emphasized separateness. I can recommend a book and a few poets who still write about it, if that would be of interest.

***

Regardless, I'm going to give you the benefit of the doubt and assume you weren't staring because I was ugly.

Maybe you were staring because you were enacting the 20-20-20 rule, which states that, if you've been looking at something for twenty minutes, put everything down, move away, get some distance. Maybe my stack of strawberry cheesecake pancakes looked especially mouth-watering. Maybe you wanted to know where my friend bought her *Harry Potter* earrings or *Star Wars* t-shirt.

Or maybe, you just weren't used to seeing a body like mine on the outside.

It's okay. None of us know what we don't know. To be fair, I didn't "know" about outsiders and insiders until someone (on the outside) told me about it.

I wish I had captured your faces, looked into your eyes. Instead, I mumbled something passive aggressive in a voice I hoped would carry and continued walking. It's okay. We don't know what we don't know.

To be fair, my mother taught me not to stare.

***

To end this letter, I'd like to share something about myself: I used to be a girl scout. Although my time only lasted two years, it was still long enough to get me into the cookie selling game.

That day at IHOP, a troop set up a table near the entrance. A dark-skinned girl asked me if I would like to buy some. I said yes, but after breakfast. I only had five dollars in cash, enough for one box. I would do anything for a child.

Children never stare. Instead, they ask questions, patiently invite answers. They are curious and without judgement. If ever we were to meet again, I hope we would be healed enough to follow their example, to recognize the teachable moment and capture it. To see the world with their eyes, wide and open.

Until then.

Allison Baldwin is a poet who combines authenticity with sass. Her work has been published most recently in The Bluebird Word. Her literary interests include lyrical and prose poems, ekphrasis and erasure, and young adult novels in verse. She holds an MFA in Poetry and Poetic Medicine from Dominican University of California and is currently developing her poetry collection, *Divining the Silhouette.*

THE BRAIN ITSELF FEELS NO PAIN

by Anita Goveas

Sometimes, when the pain made breathing stab like rusty scissors, Isha chanted random facts about the body. The body she used to have, not the fragile one she woke up to now every day, the one she was relearning. The human brain can generate enough electricity to power up a light bulb. She didn't always generate enough electricity to get out of bed; there should be a brain-powered pulley system. This journey would take so much of her energy; she needed to save some for the interview.

10% of the world were left-handed, and the world couldn't even deal with that. Was the world not made for her, or was she not made for it? So many stairs to struggle with, so many chairs that didn't seem to be for sitting in, so many unintentional touches that shuddered through her skin. Belly buttons grow special hairs just to catch lint. She could learn to curl up like a touch-me-not plant, a defence against harm. But then she might never uncurl. Defence mechanisms were something she studied at University, long nights reading about brain structures and the way it tried to heal itself.

Hazards skulked everywhere. Blushing is caused by a rush of adrenaline, like when she fell over on strangers when the bus moved too quickly. She couldn't hold on tightly enough, and she couldn't find her voice to ask for a seat. It wasn't the raising her voice that was difficult; it was the not knowing what would happen next. The contemptuous raised eyebrows, the "you look fine" pursing of the lips, the dismissive "*huh.*" She'd practised saying, "I'm disabled" in the mirror, but if her boss still expected her to fix everything, how could she convince strangers she needed help? People talked to her. That's what she did best, and she encouraged them to find ways to face their fears. It was her core, the mark she made in the world. Without that, she felt as intangible and elusive as the idea of no pain.

Isha straightened her best paisley blazer, brushed invisible dust off the knees of her pressed black trousers, pressed her nose to her wrist to inhale the jasmine she'd dabbed on. There were some things feeling every step had taught her: everyone is dealing with something, the people who were kind were not the ones you'd expect, humans are the only animals with chins, slowing down sometimes brought the dew on a leaf or the gap-toothed smile of a toddler. The line between looking professional for the Occupational Health doctor and looking like you needed no help wiggled like a fish thrashing on a hook.

Asking for help was a skill, one that she hadn't practised before she'd needed it, one that she wished she'd been eased into gradually. The human nose could detect about 1 trillion smells, more smells that it seemed a person could ever need. All of those at once would be overwhelming. She'd have to choose a skill to focus on, maybe learning to let go of her old self. She wanted to be able to explain what she needed.

Maybe easing in meant she held on tighter to things she couldn't go back to, too worried about keeping her feet on the ground while risking drowning. People who wade into the Dead Sea automatically float, more buoyant than they realise. She was a psychologist first but also a person who loved people who loved to learn. She got off the bus, plodded to the non-descript door of the office that would decide her life for the next few months. Maybe holding on was not the way forward. Maybe she could trust she would float.

Anita Goveas is British-Asian, London-based, and fuelled by strong coffee and paneer jalfrezi. She was first published in the 2016 London Short Story Prize anthology, most recently by the *Cincinnati Review*. She's on the editorial team at *Flashback Fiction* and is a submissions reader for *The Selkie*. She tweets erratically @ coffeeandpaneer. Her debut flash collection, *Families and other natural disasters*, is available from Reflex Press, and links to her stories are at https://coffeeandpaneer.wordpress.com.

WITHOUT WORDS

by Bonnie Radcliffe

For my Dad

Sounds come first. They flutter down, through the layers of sleep. Whispering. Wanting. Waking me, trying to wake me, but it is heavy darkness that I'm in here, eyes closed. It is warm, and steady, undemanding.

The sounds speed up then, gentleness gone, replaced with a beat, a swing. A repeating jumping heart. A guitar, a drum maybe, something that sounds electric. Voices, singing words I don't know, to a melody I think I do. I remember. I feel the sheet, soft from the night's warmth, brush across my back. I am moving my shoulders. I twitch my fingers. Sound. That sound… music. It's music waking me. My mouth twitches a little, yellow beat tapping its way into the dark.

Come on, darling, time to get up now.

Still, I keep my eyes shut. It is safe here, cosy. I am close to myself in the darkness, none of the gaps that keep me apart. No one asking me to remember. Your voice again, repeating itself. Your hand on my arm, gently shaking my shoulder. Still, I keep my eyes shut. The cover is pulled back, and I wince at the air. My ankles twitch. The music still plays, and I move my hands in time, and your voice comes again, a smile in it.

Time to get up.

I blink then, shaky shapes blurring, then resolving into a face, a bright room, purple curtains, a hand on my arm, one under my back, lifting me. Swivelling me to the edge of the bed.

Don't you know I can't?

Stand, come on now, on three.

Up with a lift, the world too high, my legs wobbling, then down, down again with a bump on the bed. Don't you know I can't? Why can't I be left here, where it's safe?

Again on three.

This time I wobble, almost go down, then stay there. High, held. Shaky but standing. The music still beats, and I move my hips, my hands slipping back and forth in an instinctive twist. Laughter, soft, kind, as you dance with me, then we start to move, hand under my arm, arm round my back, to the bathroom. Don't you know I can't? I know, I know I can't.

Arms raised, shirt on. Legs lifted one by one, something pulled up, then tied at my waist. Once I had all the words, but every day another skips away. Then to the stairs. The music still plays behind me, a jazzy beat, faster now. The stairs fall away in front, a gaping tunnel, a sloping drop, an impossibility. I try to sit down, but you hold me, your bent knee under me like a chair, catching my weight before you help me stand again.

One hand on the banister, you can do it.

Wood, smooth from years, beneath my palm. Dark, flat. I grip it, and it hurts, my hand so bony, veins big and blue. The other hand in yours.

One leg, one leg at a time, one small step, that's it.

I try to move my muscles, but I can't. Don't you know I can't?

That's it, that's it, you can do it. One small step down. There! There, well done.

You stay beside me, holding my hand tightly. You are always there. We go, slowly, down the stairs. You sit me at the table, silver metal—spoon—lifted to my mouth. Oatmeal and honey and nuts. Spoon sticky, never quite licked clean. I don't have the time before you take it away, dig it back into the bowl for more. Then a cup, hot, something rising from it, shapes in the air. I push it away, and you swear, jump back as hot goes everywhere. You hold my hands back, so I can't touch it, the glimmering lake, the wet.

You put my shoes on, lifting and raising my feet. You help me stand again, one two three, hold me when I wobble. Then you're zipping me into something. We're moving to the door. You turn a shiny thing, step out. Out where I can't go. Don't you know I can't?

You're further down, on the street, holding your hands out, asking me to step. I try to move forward. I try, but my foot hits the metal rim. I stop. I wobble. I can't. Why should I?

That's it, one small step down.

I stare at you. Why don't you know I can't? You hold my hand and tug gently. I dance a little, moving my hips, and you laugh.

One small step.

I can't. I can't. But you hold my hands and you wait for me and I do. I take a shaky step forward. Down. Sure, I will fall; sure, I will crash and hurt and tumble. And then I'm out and the air is warm.

Everything is green. It smells fresh and new and clean. I walk, slowly, and you hold my hand. Creatures buzz in the air, and I keep walking, slowly, but walking. There are yellow flowers and pink ones, big leaves above. Grass that waves at me. Plants I don't have names for. It is all so green. Even pushing up beneath my feet is green. Green through stone. Green on mud. You point at things and says words, names I do not remember. You smile and I do too. You point at a bush.

Look. Magnolia. Your favorite.

Creamy, thick, streaked with color, pointing to the sky. Tiny trumpets, spilling back. A smell, heady, heavy, stretching. I follow your pointing finger. I look, and it fills me up. Green and gold, white and purple, scent thick in the air and the wind on my skin. It is all okay here, where the wind blows and the flowers wave. I look at you, your smiling face, your creases. I am here; I got out. I did it, and you smile and point again.

Can't you see that, that lovely tree? Over there. Glorious. So many flowers.

Don't you know I can?

Bonnie Radcliffe is a writer based in the southeast of England. She is a keen wild swimmer and has previously written features for The Outdoor Swimming Society. She has recently completed The Mawddach Residency for emerging artists and writers and has been awarded a residency at Brisons Veor in January 2024. Her work explores storytelling and the sea, women and water, nature, daughterhood and folklore. She is currently working on a gothic novel set on a silent film set in the 1920s.

This short story explores the inherent struggles and hidden joys of being cared for as someone with Alzheimer's

ESSAYS

"NO SEAS INDIO":

RAISING AMERICAN KIDS AS A BROWN, OLIVE-SKINNED, OR NOT-WHITE-ENOUGH IMMIGRANT

by Abraham Mata

Our family loves books. In addition to learning multiple languages (we speak English, Spanish, and Romanian at home), we love to read and re-read books. Reading is our favorite pastime, after-school activity and midnight snack all rolled into one. When our son was still a baby in his highchair, he would not eat unless we read him a book while feeding him. When our daughter started reading *The Little House on the Prairie* in first grade, she would not put it down until she finished all nine volumes in less than five months. And when our kids ran out of bookshelves at the beginning of elementary school, we *had to* buy six new matching bookshelves (in addition to the three that we originally owned) to have… what was it again? Oh, yes: "room to grow." As you might guess, that didn't work: our nine bookshelves were packed neat and tight before our oldest reached the end of third grade.

The point is that we were finishing the ninth volume of *The Little House on the Prairie* when National Ranch Day came around the corner, and we decided to celebrate it by taking our little cowboy son and our little half-pint daughter to our local Ranching Heritage Center so they could learn more about pioneer life (which we thought was very appropriate for our little Texans). After reading the many trials of Laura Ingalls and her family, we had developed a great affinity for *The Little House on the Prairie*, seeing the Ingallses as very different and yet somehow similar to us: Laura's Ma and Pa were not immigrants with Ph.D.s like my wife and I, but they were also hard-working people in a far-away land, with limited resources and no extended family, and armed with tough-as-nails determination to find and build a new home. We were enjoying Ranching Day immensely, when somehow, somewhere halfway through the exhibits, something began to rub me the wrong way.

"The buffalo had their time, the Indians had their time, and now they are gone. Now is our time." – Droned the ranching guide.

I wasn't sure what it was at first, so I tried to ignore it. It felt like… an uncomfortable rock stuck inside a shoe. But that wasn't it. It was more like… an annoying fly in the middle of a sticky summer day, coming and going, giving you *besitos*, tickling you with its little *patitas* right around your ears over and over again, driving you crazy but disappearing before you could really whack it. But… that wasn't it.

"Frontier life was difficult. The Indians burned and raped." – Commented another official-looking person.

Something was bugging me, and I wasn't sure what it was. Maybe I was imagining things. Maybe I was getting paranoid. Maybe it was… *my perception*. So, I chose to focus only on the positive aspects. I paid attention to the permanent displays, appreciating that they were offered in English and Spanish (bilingualism: how nice!). I paid more attention to the featured cacti and native grasses (hello, fellow survivors!). My nose began to detect some seriously delicious barbecue and yet, somehow, I still found it difficult to concentrate.

"The Indians burned and raped… thieves… robbers… buffalo."

I saw my children listening intently to our ranching guide, and suddenly three generations of teachers in me began to detect racism and bullying. My mind started racing, and my antennas were finally up: Why were the *official* ranching guides picking on Native Americans? Were they aware of the invaluable contributions that Native Americans provided to ciboleros, rancheros, vaqueros and cowboys all over the Plains? Why were they describing them as rapists and thieves? And since teachers are (or should be) the natural predators of bullies, I zeroed in on the source of abuse, and yet, as our guide concluded his remarks, I hesitated.

Those were not my people, I thought to myself. I should not get involved. I'm barely even brown! Why should I say anything? No one else seemed to care, and I did not want to make my white wife uncomfortable. Why not just ignore it? Why not just look the other way…?

"The *Indians*…"

And then I saw my father's face in a half-remembered conversation I had with him many years ago: "*Nunca te burles de los indios. Si algún día sientes ganas de insultar a alguien diciéndole «¡eres un indio!», recuerda que tu padre es un indio, y que tú llevas sangre azteca también. ¡Nunca te avergüences de tus ancestros!*" (Never make fun of Native Americans. If you ever feel like insulting anyone by telling them "You are an Indian!" remember that your father is an *indio*, and that you carry Aztec blood as well. Never be ashamed of your ancestors!). And so, I leaned over to my mixed-blood children and told them out loud, in English, so that other people could understand us:

"*Los indios* were not as horrible as they are trying to make you think. They were people with families and children, like you or me. They were angry because they were driven from their ancestral homes. Remember we are standing on stolen land. Remember your father has Native American blood as well."

"Yes Pa!," my children replied.

Or maybe it was something like "Ok. That's nice. Let's go find a jackrabbit." Oh, well. We moved on, my children had a wonderful time, they did manage to see a jackrabbit or two, and I think we even took them for ice cream afterwards. But I kept stewing. Had I done enough? I didn't think so. The Ph.D.-wielding idealistic university professor, former missionary in me felt eager to have some firm words with the organizers of the event. And yet, my crusty, jaded, tough-as-nails, practical immigrant side remained unconvinced: Why waste my time? I am a highly skilled American professor, and so what? If I just reach out to the organizers, are they really going to listen to *me*? After 20 years in the U.S., I still do not belong. My own church people still ask me, "Where are you from? No, *really*, where are you from *originally*?" I am not white enough to pass as white, my American accent is now too thick to go unnoticed in Mexico, and I don't have the right blood quantum to count as Native American in the U.S. Why preach to those who will not listen?

And that's when it hit me: mexicano, hispano, latino, chicano, pocho, malinchista, vendepatria. *Indio*. M'ijo, m'ija, hermano, brother, sister. Friend. *La raza de bronce*. Being a brown, tanned, olive-skinned, or (not) white-enough-immigrant can be quite complicated. Some who can pass by white, do so, but either way, you become "ni de aquí ni de allá." Not from here, not from there, not from anywhere. Home becomes a blurry concept. Sometimes you end up with American parents in addition to your biological ones. Sometimes your family in your country of origin forgets you, but you cultivate a new one here. Sometimes, you discover that your sweet late *abuelita* was a wonderful, compassionate, and racist white woman who ended up marrying a Native American man. Sometimes the inconsistencies, glaring ironies, and constant drama of your own life befuddle you, and you begin to wonder if in fact your own life couldn't be the plot of some crazy *telenovela*.

Sometimes you experience terrible discrimination, and then make great efforts so your children don't become hard and jaded like you. Sometimes, you discover you've been racist against *indios* yourself… pretending to be 100% Spaniard when in fact more than half of your *ancestros* come from the original inhabitants of the Americas. Sometimes, you look at your psychologist in the eyes, and wonder how on earth they are going to understand what you've been through.

Sometimes, your children say "Ai plej aliyance tu the flak" without truly understanding it. And then you swell with pride as you explain that United States is their home, and then, together, you learn the pledge of allegiance and the anthem, compete with one another to see who sings it better and more passionately, and teach them that they must always do their best to make America even more beautiful than it already is.

…I think I am going to write a letter to the organizers of the event after all.

Dr. Abraham Mata is Associate Professor of Spanish and Portuguese at Lubbock Christian University, where he also serves as Foreign Languages Program Coordinator and head of the Spanish Education Program. A Hispanic professor with Nahua, Mexican and Spanish ancestry, he gained valuable insights into the struggles of immigrants, refugees, and other minorities through his personal experience migrating to the United States.

In his narrative above, he provides a glimpse into the everyday challenges of raising two multi-ethnic Texan children as a not-white-enough immigrant struggling with racism and discrimination.

MOTHER TONGUE:

A MEDITATION ON ASIAN SILENCE

by Daniel

In the face of Trump's anti-Asian pandemic rhetoric, and especially after the Atlanta spa shootings, it seemed the AAPI community had found its voice. Our growing boldness to speak up found its culmination in the 2023 Oscars, when *Everything Everywhere All at Once* swept seven awards, and we finally felt like our stories were worth telling ("Ke Huy Quan Wins").

Every second Ke Huy Quan went over time on his acceptance speech, we kept thinking he was building up the courage to tell *his* story, the one we were all waiting to hear: how he spent thirty years waiting for a call that never came, how Hollywood didn't believe anyone cared for AAPI narratives. Instead, he waxed poetic about the American Dream—the golden calf of the model minority mythos. The whole world was listening, and he preached the opiate of the masses that, in America, if one worked hard enough, they could achieve anything. He said this as Angela Bassett watched on, and in front of the TV, my undocumented brother, who fears deportation daily, sighed—while my citizen brother muttered something about how Bassett would not have stayed silent and how the black experience understands the American Dream is *copium*[1].

Just a few years ago, I watched officer Tao shield Derek Chauvin. My citizen brother described the scene of Floyd's murder as an allegory of race relations in America. It did not surprise me that Tao, an Asian-American, stood in defense of racial oppression. His actions were the logical direction of a culture of shame and silence. We are a people that, when faced with the deck stacked against us, put up with it. We suffer from a chronically excessive internal locus of control.

---

1 Internet slang for a story one tells themselves as a coping mechanism.

Officer Tao. *Tao*. It's the common transliterated spelling for 道, that East Asian philosophy Westerners call *the way*. One of its central tenets is *wuwei* or *inaction/inexertion*. We're all familiar with Bruce Lee's "water in a cup" metaphor: "Be like water making its way through cracks. Do not be assertive, but adjust to the object, and you shall find a way around or through it" (@brucelee). Like water, we're bent and curved by our surroundings, playing along with the system.

Asian-Americans "are the least likely to hold elected office" (Dugyala). We have "one of the most dismal voter turnout rates" (Kim). Why are we silent? I cannot speak for all that is *we*. [2] But I can begin by telling you why I was silent. It was because of our mothers and our mouths. And I can tell of how I found hope in the mirror.

---

2 Before I go further, I want to point out that the AAPI community is not a monolith; we are, in fact, one of the most diverse racial demographics. We have the highest economic disparity within our race, the most diverse religious makeup, and varied political allegiances. Thus, I am writing out of my own lived experience as a Malaysian-Chinese immigrant who arrived in Abilene, TX at the age of 17. I am writing, too, out of my brothers' embodied stories: My eldest brother is a native-born citizen. My second eldest brother is undocumented. My youngest brother still resides in our home country. By family order: a citizen, an illegal immigrant, a legal immigrant, and a foreigner—we're a case study waiting to happen.

Mothers

In Amy Tan's *Joy Luck Club*, Waverly Jong embarrasses her mother by lashing out at her in public and running away. When Waverly returns, prepared for her mother to reprimand her in fury, she instead finds a dinner table shrouded in silence. Her mother has forbidden her family from speaking to her. She discovers that this, which seems like no punishment, is a fate worse than a violent verbal outburst.

We were taught to respond to suffering with silence. In all its forms.

In Malaysia, when we drove past traffic accidents, our mothers made us children look away. My mother seemed to think that spirits would float from under the black sheets and fly into our eyes. If we looked at scenes of violence, ghosts would follow us in our heads.

Sometimes the accidents were more inconvenient than tragic, and our mothers would sigh quietly at the bottlenecking, reminding their children in the back to not be busy bodies. *Don't be a busy body*, we schoolchildren chanted, whenever some nosy person was sticking their nose somewhere it didn't belong. *Mind your own business*—that was the slogan of my Southeast Asian upbringing.

We were taught to turn away—to sit down and shut up. My mother thought that *shut up* was a bad word. Instead, she said, *If you have nothing good to say, don't say it.* And *nothing good* included protesting any injustice or expressing our suffering.

My youngest brother reminds us of how, when he once fell down an escalator and tore up his knee, my mother's first reaction was an imperative, *Don't cry*.

Mouths

We are afraid to speak too because of our bodies—the shape of our mouths. My undocumented brother once lamented the fact that the biology of the Chinese tongue prevents full mastery of the white American accent. I was, of course, skeptical of this at first. *I am simply not trying hard enough*, I told myself, but soon, I came across an article about Asian parents arranging lingual frenectomies for their children (Demick).

But I've never needed an article to tell me the tongue is the strongest muscle, struggling against my pronunciations—a wall between me and the *you* I am trying to speak to. I can adopt some of the most high-brow vocabulary of the Standard American Dialect (SAD), yet my friends stop me in the middle of our conversations with laughter and *Did you means. Did you mean to say* "də-ˈle-mə"*? I've just never heard it said that way before.*

In *On Earth We're Briefly Gorgeous*, Little Dog writes of his family's quest for oxtail at the butcher's, of how the employees laugh at his mother's attempts to explain oxtail by pantomime—his mother want of words making finger horns on her head. This is the moment that Vuong resolves to learn words, to speak for his family.

Like Little Dog, I hide behind my writing: On this blank white page, tell me, can I not be white to you too? In 12-point Times New Roman, I sashay my perfectly punctuated clauses, with no red squiggly underlines or places you may pause to say, *Come again?* Truthfully, I do not need you to think I'm white, only that you do not think about this at all, that I am another disembodied voice—that I am Ralph Waldo Emerson's "transparent eyeball."

But for us the unmarked voice is an impossibility. In my first day subbing in a middle school classroom, I was greeted by a sixth-grader's loud burst of *ching-chong*, followed by class after class of students wanting to know where I was from. It got to the point I prepared a bellringer script:

Good morning! You may have already noticed that I don't sound like I'm from here. Well, that's because I'm not. I'm from a country called Malaysia.

So when Suresh Canagarajah and Geneva Smitherman advocate translingualism—the notion that teaching SAD is racist, my first instinct is to cry out, *Please don't take this from me too—the only hill I've conquered* (Jackson et al.). I may never look or sound "American," but let me hide, at least, behind my skin of text. Still, I know this is my privilege.

In a grad class, we discussed CCCC's resolution "Students' Right to Their Own Language" (SRTOL) (Jackson et al.). The professor, who happened to be the director of the writing center, pointed out that second-language speakers who visit the center have always asked to be taught SAD and that the center was obligated to fulfill this need. As the token minority in the room, I was obligated to respond; I informed him that, personally, I too longed to be taught the right/white way to write; however, I must acknowledge that my status as an immigrant predisposes me to desire assimilation—regardless of its violence upon my identity.

While I am frustrated by Emerson's ability to exist unmarked, Li-Young Lee, in "The

Cleaving," criticizes Emerson for writing that the Chinese have "managed to preserve to a hair / for three or four thousand years / the ugliest features in the world." *Comic ugliness* is the status that Western media has bestowed upon all Asian accents for centuries. But we are not absolved of blame; at times, faced with scarcity of roles in media, Asians have opted to inhabit the role of Asian minstrel. Recently, many have called out Malaysian comedian, Nigel Ng, for furthering racist stereotypes through his "Uncle Roger" persona (Wolseley).

Still, I understand the faux allure of minstrelsy. While my citizen brother had striven for white adjacence, and my undocumented brother had pushed back against anti-Asian hate, I, as a freshman international student, leaned into the tropes, hoping to pawn my Asian minstrelsy to make friends.

So, when an American student asked me to entertain him with an Asian accent, I obliged. I was told that my comic Asian accent was terrible, so I endeavored to master the stereotypical Chinglish accent. For most of my undergrad years, I transformed my body into the butt of Asian jokes and tropes, wearing rice hats and cracking jokes about eating domestic animals.

But this had a price I couldn't see at the time. It wasn't until years later, when I first met Li-Young Lee's poetry, that I finally realized the toll that my minstrelsy had taken on me—on all who looked like me.

Mirrors

For years, if my writing ever took on a political subject, it was to decry racial violence against black and brown bodies; I could never write about my own embodied experience. I questioned my place as marginalized: *What do I know of racial oppression? I have never feared for my life at a traffic stop or felt my heart leap at every door knock.* Whenever it came to speaking of my own marked body, I was the fish in Lee's poem, "three pounds of dumb / nerve and pulse."

Similarly, Asian underrepresentation in the media had not bothered me, nor the English literary canon's absence of marginalized voices. To study English meant studying English culture, and I assumed its monolithic nature came with the territory. Then, I encountered Lee's poetry.

I met him across *The City in Which I Love You* and saw, in his lines, my own face. When he sings of his lover and her "inverted fountain in which [he does] not see [himself]," I recognized instantly that she was simultaneously his lover and white America. For all my love for this new country, I—on my knees, face buried between her hips—could not see me.

In "The Cleaving," Lee sees himself in a Chinese butcher, writing "this man with my face." And as he describes this man's "Gobi, Northern" visage, "its boniness / clear from the high / warlike forehead / to the sheer edge of the jaw," I find myself transformed into the butcher. This is a love poem Lee has written for me—for us, the ones who have managed to preserve to a hair our *ugliest features in the world*.

His poems awakened in me a desire to embrace home—and I began to write of my own struggles with assimilating into American culture, confronting discomforts I had heretofore swept under the rug. In the face of all the shame and silence we grew up in, he taught me to love my body, and consequently, my voice, by writing of his unloved body, and I discovered that the marked body is itself a gift. Because your body is no longer made of dust but of story, and you must look in the mirror and see that it is beautiful, that it is a story worth telling.

Works Cited

@brucelee. "Be like water making its way through cracks. Do not be assertive, but adjust to the object, and you shall find a way around or through it. If nothing within you stays rigid, outward things will disclose themselves." *Twitter*, 2 May 2020, 5:00 a.m., https://twitter.com/brucelee/status/1256523890102341635?lang=en.

Demick, Barbara. "Some in S. Korea Opt for a Trim When English Trips the Tongue." *Los Angeles Times*, 31 March 2002, www.latimes.com/archives/la-xpm-2002-mar-31-mn-35590-story.html.

Dugyala, Rishika. "Asian Americans are the least likely to hold elected office." *Politico*, 4 May 2021, www.politico.com/news/2021/05/04/asian-american-pacific-islander-representation-elected-office-485279.

Emerson, Ralph Waldo. *Nature*. Penguin, 1982.

Jackson, Austin, et al. *Students' Right to Their Own Language: A Critical Sourcebook*. Bedford/St. Martin's, 2014.

"Ke Huy Quan Wins Best Supporting Actor for 'Everything Everywhere All at Once' | 95th Oscars (2023)." *YouTube*, uploaded by Oscars, 11 Apr. 2023, https://www.youtube.com/watch?v=EZ1SUKxSAi4.

Kim, Caitlin. "Why Asian Americans Don't Vote." *New America*, 7 Sep. 2017, www.newamerica.org/weekly/why-asian-americans-dont-vote/.

Lee, Li-Young. *The City in Which I Love You*. BOA, 1990.

Tan, Amy. *The Joy Luck Club*. Penguin, 1989.

Vuong, Ocean. *On Earth We're Briefly Gorgeous*. Penguin, 2019.

Wolseley, Kat. "Why Uncle Roger's throwaway racism can do real damage." Hong Kong Free Press, 24 Jan. 2021, hongkongfp.com/2021/01/24/why-uncle-rogers-throwaway-racism-can-do-real-damage/.

Drawing on my family's embodied experiences as Malaysian-Chinese immigrants, I discuss the complex relationship between suffering, silence, and voice in our culture—further complicated by the fact that our bodies are situated within the context of the white American south. I address two sources of silence—our familial upbringing and our biology. I discuss representation as a balm.

LINEN CLOSETS

by Rachel Lutwick-Deaner

At one point, my memoir almost had one of these titles:

- Little Jewish Star of Bethlehem: A Loaf of Rye Bread in a Wonder Bread Town
- Nice Jewish Girls Eat Pork Barbeque: A North Carolina Reverie
- Just a Reminder, They're Coming for Me First: Confronting My Community About White Supremacists
- Pickled Lox with Cream Sauce: My Girlhood of Bagels and Appetizing
- Chocolate Chip Bagels Are a Crime Against Nature: And Other Lessons Only Your Jewish Friends Will Tell You
- Jews Don't Walk on Train Tracks: Facts About the People of the Book That You Never Knew
- Her Face Is Like a Map of Jerusalem

But recently I'm quite fond of:

- Realtors, Show Me Your Linen Closets: I'm Going to Need to Hide My Family in There

As these titles would suggest, being Jewish is a big part of my identity. So is food, but food is a big part of being Jewish. Matzo balls, challah, latkes, brisket, rugelach, I could go on forever. But living as a Jewish woman in America is more complicated than food, and it's not as fun to talk about.

A notable part of my Jewish identity is anxiety. Anxiety about making it into the Book of Life on Yom Kippur. Anxiety about taking off of work or not on the High Holy Days. Anxiety about whether or not it's a good choice to visit Israel for 10 days (Hamas! The PLO! Will my family be able to feed themselves?). There's lots of Holocaust anxiety.

I admit, somewhat meekly, that I have spent an inordinate part of my life considering where and how I would hide from the Nazis. When I share this with my Jewish friends, they nod, knowingly. Cathy says that she and Mark talk about who would turn them into the Gestapo (it's that grouchy neighbor down the street). Tracy says that she was careful not to let her passport expire, you know, "Just in case."

Lest you think this is just the neurosis of middle aged women, consider Nathan Englander's 2011 short story, "What We Talk About When We Talk About Anne Frank." Englander depicts two Jewish couples, old friends, who get high and wind up playing a game or "not a game. It's just what we talk about when we talk about Anne Frank," in which they assess one another for their capabilities as a "Righteous Gentile." Essentially, if one of the spouses was not Jewish, would s/he hide the others? What a question, right? But as a Jewish person in America, in a post-Holocaust world, it's an important one to ask. And I don't have to get high to think about it.

Growing up, I thought a lot about hiding, thanks to the frightening world of children's Holocaust literature. In elementary school, we did a read aloud of *Twenty and Ten* by Claire Hutchet Bishop. This book forgoes the horrors of gas chambers and burial pits, instead focusing on the narrative of twenty French children, sent to the countryside, presumably out of harm's way, with their teacher, a nun. These twenty children are asked to hide ten Jewish children.

The twenty French children hid the ten Jewish children in a cave in the woods. They contorted their bodies into a barely visible crack in the rock face, through which they found a cavernous interior fit for waiting out the Nazis. The ink-drawn illustration showed a cave that was dark but roomy and dry. And they brought snacks.

From *Twenty and Ten*, I immersed myself in the genre. *The Cigarette Sellers*, *The Endless Steppe*, *The Upstairs Room*, *The Summer of My German Soldier*, *When Hitler Stole the Pink Rabbit*, *Uncle Mischa's Partisans*. With relish, I read a junior version of the *Rise of Adolph Hitler*. I don't know that I understood most of the horrors these books described. My takeaway was the need to plan out a hiding place.

I loved to hide under my white Formica desk, built into the blocky furniture of my girlhood room. Tucking a blanket into the desk drawer, I could nestle into the cavern, just big enough for me and a friend. I could sometimes tote my infant sister in there too, but it was hard to maintain silence when I was awkwardly clutching a newborn. Years later, holding a screaming infant during those early post-partum weeks, I would remember what hiding Jews had to do to silence their crying babies. I was haunted by the image of pouring water down their throats to drown them and save the group. But as a child, I didn't yet know that particular horror. I merely assessed that under the desk was too crowded; the blanket in the desk drawer was too obvious to fool the SS, so I considered the linen closet.

The linen closet in my childhood home was a place no one could hide. We had just one, in our split-level house on Long Island. There was no way we were getting even one of us in there. You were lucky to find a matching set of sheets. Stuffed next to my sister's lavender and chintz crib bumper and matching baby quilt was the top sheet from my brother's Pac Man sheet set. The flannel top sheets, reminiscent of the Toronto hospitals where my mother did her nurses' training, were packed so tightly that they seemed to give off the heat of the dryer weeks after they had been stored away. The washcloth tower had slid underneath the extra bathmats and the extra large beach towels emblazoned with "Chocosaurus" and the Mets insignia. There was not a spare inch for a person who wanted to hide–not an extra breath of fresh air for the frightened lurker behind the shelves.

If only I had some stairs behind a bookcase.

Reading *The Diary of Anne Frank* (both abridged and unabridged) over the course of my childhood impressed me in one way: Damn! They were lucky. That stairway behind the bookcase? What a boon! That place was big! With windows! Haven't you heard of other people who spent their hiding years in barns? Cellars? Closets? Underground? Anne Frank had it made. Before they closed it off to tourists, I stood in that room behind the stairs, furtively peeking at the apartment buildings across the way, appreciating the bold blue sky that seemed indulgent, given the circumstances of other, less fortunate, Jews in hiding.

I have met people, usually young people, who will tell me that *The Diary of Anne Frank* is their favorite book. Their favorite. I know. Maybe they haven't read much. I have to assume that part of the affinity they feel for the book is that it's completely foreign to them—similar to reading a post-apocalyptic book—they've never had to think about hiding because someone wants to kill you and your family—your entire people. Dara Horn's astute *People Love Dead Jews* reveals another reason the Western World loves Anne Frank so much. Horn argues that Jews are most treasured when we are powerless, dead for moments or generations, that people love us when our existence reflects their own goodness, piety, as is the case with *The Diary of Anne Frank*. And Anne is the perfect dead Jew; she absolves humanity of their role in her death, noting, "I believe, in spite of everything, that people are truly good at heart." As Horn points out, these words "flatter us."

Of course, Anne Frank didn't know her fate, Auschwitz and Bergen-Belsen, didn't really understand the scope of the genocide, so maybe it was easier for her to believe in the goodness of people. This year, Anne would have turned 94. I wonder if she would still feel the same way? Or if she would spend her time shifting quilts around in the linen closet or reimaging storage space in the garage?

Englander's fictional friends play their Holocaust game after the host couple illustrate that the pantry and downstairs bathroom could be walled off as a hiding place, a full service shelter, if need be, in case, *just in case*, they had to hide from the Nazis. If survival during a second Holocaust here in America depends on the plausibility of building a hidden room, I'm considering my options.

Post-Tree of Life shooting, I had a passing conversation with my neighbor, a native of the

Netherlands (*there's a hint right there*) about a rental property he owns in a beach town nearby. Our families were planning to meet at this home, and my friend mentioned where I could find the key if we arrived before he did.

He said, "I keep a spare key under the doormat."

I heard: *You can use our house if the Nazis come to Grand Rapids*.

My suspicions were further confirmed when this friend graciously showed me the "private" areas of the rental—rooms that stayed locked when visitors took ownership of the house for a week or two.

He said: "When I'm not using the space, I lock up my office and the kids' bedroom."

I heard: "These private rooms—*hiding places*—are there to house families such as yours, when the time comes, because after all, our president is Donald Trump."

My family will definitely depend on the kindness of those few righteous gentiles, because my old house is not a great hiding place at all. Storming through our 1920's "English Arts-and-Crafts" house, flamethrowers poised, the Nazis would find the five of us immediately. There's no way we could all squeeze into the downstairs half bath. We don't have a pantry. And, like my girlhood linen closet, the linen closets are so stuffed with sheets and expired over-the-counter medications, we couldn't even get our dog in there. We did convert our attic into a third floor living space, but unlike the fleet footed Frank family, our hippopotamic foot falls would give us away immediately. Not one of my children can walk up the stairs or shut a door without the entire house shaking like a 4.8 point earthquake. And even though there is unfinished storage space, we'd do ourselves in before being marched off to the camps. Each one of us has allergies so dramatic that the dust would choke us first–a mercy perhaps? We should have done a new build and put in a stairway behind a bookcase.

In my darkest moments, I look at my children and assess how Jewish they really look. They do look like "regular white people," I think, but there's a coarse quality to my oldest daughter's hair, despite her peaches and cream complexion and flashing blue eyes. My son, freckled and similarly blue eyed, yes, but there's something vaguely semitic about the curve of his nose. Could someone pick it out? My youngest, though. She could fool them all. She has stick-straight blond hair and green eyes. She's thin and rangy, where our people tend to be curvy and soft. If they lined us up, I know I would be a lost cause. My face *is* a map of Jerusalem. The older two as well, I fear. But the baby—she might just make it. Hiding in plain sight.

We're already hiding in plain sight. All the years when you couldn't find a box of matzah at the store at Passover? The holiday concerts with no whisper of a Hanukkah song? The eternal question, "What is your home church?" Is this a way to live? How do I want to live? On one hand, if people don't see us, we don't have to build out that staircase behind the bookshelf because we're safe–safe enough. But as Dara Horn points out, in the shadow of Tree of Life and many other crimes against Jewish communities, "Our cherished belief in America as an exception in Jewish History might be a delusion." And if that's the case, I'd very much like a roomy linen closet. Just to be safe.

Rachel Lutwick-Deaner is an emerging writer, college professor, mother, and ruminator, living in the Midwest. I earned a BA in English from Colgate University, and an MA in English Literature from North Carolina State University. I recently completed my MFA in Creative

Nonfiction at Queens University of Charlotte. My as-yet-unpublished essay collection, "Unmentionables: Reflections from a (Not So) Nice Midwestern Lady" asks the reader to contemplate identity, through the lens of family, memory, language, motherhood, womanhood, and individuality. You can find me on Instagram @professor.ld.

I NEVER GOT TO PLAY THE OREGON TRAIL

by C. Kohrs

I've never been very good at math or staying on task. If all my classmates' assignments were turned in for the quarter, they were rewarded with viewings of The Nightmare Before Christmas in the gym. If they finished all their classwork on time, they played *The Oregon Trail* at the end of the school day. I listened to them giggle and laugh, bragging about who died from dysentery the least. I stared at my crumpled-up sheets of math problems struggling to understand and complete the homework I "lost."

When I was six, I found uncompleted math worksheets shoved in the back of my perpetually messy desk. The following year, I proudly told my first-grade teacher, "Now that I'm in second grade, I don't shove my homework in the back of my desk anymore." Two months later, my new teacher, Mrs. Sours, reprimanded me for missing work.

On a Monday morning, I handed my teacher a *Lion King* coloring page.

"I colored this just for you, Mrs. Sours," I said.

"You didn't color in the lines, Cassie." She frowned and pushed my artwork back to me. I went to my seat and shoved it in the back of my desk.

Occasionally, students read stories out loud to the class. I wanted to read *Stellaluna* by Janell Cannon. I was mesmerized by the beautiful illustrations. The book was published the year before and had just hit our school library's shelves. It took weeks for me to get my hands on a copy.

Finally, the day came. It was my turn to read *Stellaluna*. I opened the first page.

"In a wa-warm and sul-try for-for-est far, far, away there once lived a mo-moth-er fru-it bat and her new bay-bee—"

"Cassie," Mrs. Sours said. "If this book is too complicated for you, you never should have volunteered to read." She'd never interrupted any of the other kids.

"I can do it," I said. "I just—"

"No," my teacher said. "You're done for today. Sit back down. Next time, pick a book you know you can read." I hung my head, slowly slid off the chair, and returned to my spot on the floor. I picked at the carpet while the next kid read their selection. When I returned to my desk, I shoved the book to the back of my desk. I didn't look at it again until it was due.

Later that year, I was at a table outside of my classroom. My parents were talking to Mrs. Sours and someone I didn't know. I colored *Clifford the Big Red Dog* outside the lines while they spoke in low voices. Eventually, I was called into the room. Someone explained that I had a learning disability and things would be better now because I would attend Ms. Hogan's class.

She seemed like fun. She taught my friends Nathan and Josh. Sometimes she stopped and said hi to me because she knew my big brother and asked about him.

Being in "Special Ed" didn't have a sting to it yet because Ms. Hogan didn't make me feel like I was different from anyone else. I didn't have to try to impress her. She just helped me.

"Cassie, you wrote 'to' here instead of 'too.' Do you understand why that's wrong?"

I shook my head no.

"The word *T-W-O* is a number. You have *two* pencils. *T-O-O* is a measurement. That pencil is *too* small, or that pencil is *too* far away. It can stand in for *also* as well. I like that pencil *too*. Making sense so far?"

I nodded.

"*T-O* tells you where something is going. I am going *to* sharpen the pencil."

I colored a picture of Timon and Pumbaa from *The Lion King*. She taped it on the wall behind her desk.

The following year, third graders gathered around the TV every Friday to watch *Ghostwriter* and *Bill Nye the Science Guy*. The special ed kids went downstairs to practice writing in cursive. I never got to see an episode.

Taking classes with Ms. Hogan instead of with the normal kids helped me tremendously. I would have been held back if it hadn't been for my diagnosis. Still, I was never an honor roll student. I was lucky if I got a C+ in any of my classes. No matter how hard I worked, I couldn't finish my assignments in time to do the fun things the smart kids did.

That's why it's weird to me when people my age talk about the happy memories *The Oregon Trail* brings them. That's not my experience because it was a privilege. In fifth grade, I did get to be a smart kid once. I finished my classwork for the day, and for five glorious minutes, I died of dysentery twice.

C. Kohrs is a writer and a business owner. She graduated from the University of Cincinnati with a bachelor's degree in creative writing. Her poem "Splinter," published under Cassie Saines, can be found in *Ohio Bards Poetry Anthology*. She lives in Cincinnati with her husband, son, and three pets.

I SOLEMNLY SWEAR

THAT I AM UP TO NO GOOD

by Leighton Schreyer

The witch's hat was like any other mass-produced costume accessory, which is to say that it was cheap; made of flimsy nylon fabric; crinkled, still, from who knows how long it had been stashed in the closet with Snow White and Cinderella and all the other Halloween costumes my sister and I had begged and thrown temper tantrums for, then swiftly forgotten about, the ways little kids do. A few days earlier, however, in anticipation of September 1st (Hogwart's Day), my sister had dug that big, black witch hat out of the closet. She'd snipped off the spiderwebs laced around its brim and furrowed its crinkles into a frown and, on September 1st at precisely 11 o'clock, she'd ordered me to charge straight through her bedroom door (Platform 9 ¾). Dutifully, I did—I always did.

Safely in the Wizarding World, we boarded the Hogwarts Express together and busied ourselves gossiping about Hagrid and Snape, McGonagall and Mad Eye Moody. She introduced me to Licorice Wands and Chocolate Frogs and dared me to different colours of Bertie Botts Every Flavour Beans (rotten egg is the worst). Later, we baked Pumpkin Pasties and sipped Butter Beer and, when all snacks had been sampled, she taught me spells, helped me to perfect the swish and flick of my wand. When we arrived at Hogwarts, my sister pointed me to the old, tripod wooden stool in the middle of her room and placed the witch's hat on my head.

"Ahhhhh, right then," she mused philosophically, her voice deep and booming from the closet where she hid. "Hmmm, very difficult. Veeeeery difficult, indeed. Not a bad mind. A bit of courage, too. Lots of ambition, yes. Where to put you?" My heart raced, palms sweating, as if I was actually waiting to be sorted into a house—to have my whole life laid out befor me, my entire character summed up by a label. A name. Some stereotype or cliché.

"I wonder…" She was purposefully prolonging the torture, at this point. "Yes, that's it! HUFFLEPUFF!"

Hufflepuff: it was her version of an insult, I thought—that good 'ol sisterly love. Everyone (and I mean everyone) knew Hufflepuff was the house for those not brave enough for Gryffindor, ambitious enough for Slytherin, or smart enough for Ravenclaw. Simply Other. Like the runt of the litter, Hufflepuff was reserved for those who didn't fit in, who had nothing (or at least not much) going for them. The ones who, presumably, no one wanted. There were no characters from Hufflepuff who advanced the plot, no scenes of any significance sporting bumblebee-coloured stripes. I mean, their mascot was a badger. Their existence was trivial.

I knew better than to argue with the sorting hat, though. While it didn't always say what people wanted to hear, it said what it knew to be true.

That year, we played Quidditch in the backyard and disappeared under invisibility cloaks. We turned back time, made potions, and fought Dementors. In the mornings, as we hustled around the house packing lunch bags and gym bags and backpacks with three different pairs of shoes, my sister and I took turns asking each other, "Ready Freddy?" and answering with an impassioned, "Ready George!" When the school year was over, we ran home cheering, "Dobby is a free elf!" We exchanged textbooks for spell books and practiced properly enunciating our words (it's leviOsa, not levioSA, in case you're wondering).

This all-encompassing imaginative play was nothing new. My sister had a track record of losing herself in fantasy worlds (and pulling me along with her). It started with *Sailor Moon* when she was seven, an obsession my parents quickly tried to quell by hiding her VHS tape and pink plastic moon stick, hoping that would be enough to bring her back to reality. And it was. But only temporarily. She returned to our world only long enough to let her disgruntlement be known, then plunged straight into the Pokémon world. Eventually, Pokémon gave way to Avatar and Avatar to Percy Jackson, which was followed by Star Wars before (I don't think I missed anything) landing on Harry Potter. In any case, the Wizarding World was the last world my sister lost herself in. The last fantasy one, at least. Soon after leaving Hogwarts a fully qualified wizard, my sister traded those age-old books for an even older one: the Bible. Christian Doctrine began dictating her life and, before I even knew what was happening, I lost her again. This time to God.

Nearly ten years later, on the cusp of my twenty-first birthday, I came out as trans. I don't know what compelled me to tell my sister first, but I did. Maybe I was trying to do the hardest thing first, to get the worst out of the way. Or maybe it was my way of testing the waters, of understanding how safe it was for me to tell the truth, to get a sense of how much I had to lose. Regardless, it was my sister to whom I first recited the script I had spent weeks stumbling through in my head.

I tried explaining how unsettled I felt in my body, how nothing ever felt quite right. I explained how I'd tried to be the person everyone wanted me to be, the person they expected me to be, the one they told me I was. But the truth, I said, was that that wasn't me. Hiding that truth was starting to become suffocating. I couldn't do it anymore. I needed to come up for air. I told her my name was Leighton, my pronouns: he/him.

She asked if she could pray for me. God made me a woman, she said, and God doesn't make mistakes. She told me her first and greatest commandment was to love the Lord her Father with all her heart, which she wouldn't be doing if she used he/him pronouns to refer to me or thought of me as her brother. In fact, doing so would be to deny God's truth, her truth, the only truth, in her mind. It would be a disgrace. I could pretend to be a man, she said. But I would never *be* a man. Not a real one, at least.

Just like that, I was erased from this world, transported into a fictional world of my own. Who knew all that time spent in the Wizarding World in my past would come back to haunt me in the future? That, after all those years of me stepping into her world—of riding broomsticks and running through doors, of chasing Pikachu and drawing arrows on my head, learning how to air-bend and water-bend and trying my best to fire-bend—that, after all that time, she would be unwilling to step into my world, unwilling to gender-bend.

Trust me, trans folks have heard it all: we're imposters, fraudsters, evil deceivers, and make believers. Our lives are a pretense just waiting to crumble; our existence, a fabrication already bursting at its seams. Our identities are treated as illusions that, with the swish and flick of a wand, can appear—*swish, flick*—and disappear. Woman—*swish, flick*—man. Man—*swish, flick*—woman. Swish and flick, swish and flick, swish and flick. Always with the binary. Sooner or later, our act will come to an end. It's just a matter of time, they say.

These are the beliefs that lead people to call the cops on us, to charge us on account of "False Personation" and have us arrested for "Sexual Fraud" or "Genderfucking Non-Disclosure." These are the beliefs that lead people to pull guns on us, citing panic in their defense, as if it's acceptable—rational, even—to kill someone based on their gender identity. They suggest it's our fault, their violence. That we chose this for ourselves by "choosing" to be trans. These are the beliefs that lead people to cheer as states outlaw drag performances. "To protect our children," they say, when it's the trans children whose lives are truly at peril. Our lives don't matter—it's not like we even existed in the first place.

Sometimes, when I feel lost and alone and am afraid of being seen, I wonder if I would be better able to navigate this fictitious world I'm inhabiting if I had paid more attention when my sister pulled out the Marauder's Map, all those years ago. If I would know where to go to escape Filch's patrol, or what spell to say to make myself visible again, to have my voice heard again, to make my life matter again. Who knows? Maybe I would. But honestly, I doubt it because no matter how much time I spend in the Wizarding World, I will never be a wizard. My life is not an illusion. My identity is real. My existence is valid. And not until that is realized—not until trans rights are honoured and upheld, not until our lives are celebrated and our identities respected—will I close my Marauders Map and say: "mischief managed."

Leighton Schreyer (they/them) is a writer, poet, and critically Mad queer activist in Toronto, ON, whose writing often explores themes of gender, sexuality, mental health, and the human condition. Their work has been featured in some of the world's leading medical and literary journals, including *The Sun*, *The New England Journal of Medicine*, *Journal of the American Medical Association*, *Hippocampus Magazine*, *Redivider*, and more. Their writing has been nominated for The Pushcart Prize. As a current medical student, Leighton is passionate about recentering the fundamental role that story plays in healthcare and caregiving, and about using narrative as a powerful tool to foster healing and human connection.

A LAW AGAINST ONE IS A LAW AGAINST US ALL:

A BRIEF OVERVIEW ON HOW ANTI-LGBTQIA LEGISLATION IMPACTS THE COMMUNITY AS A WHOLE

by Theresa Bernesser

Many of us remember how our schooling and the support groups we found there shaped our identities, our own self-esteem and had lasting impacts that we carry on into our everyday lives. Imagine being in a stage of your life where you begin to question who you're attracted to, how you identify and then those things being regarded with a hush-hush attitude that makes you feel ashamed. This is the impact recent legislative measures can carry in youth of varying LGBTQIA identities.

A recent article from CNN[3] names different bills that are being presented in government to prevent the discussions of sexual orientation and gender with these examples,

"An Iowa bill that passed the state House last week that would prohibit instruction about gender identity and sexual orientation from kindergarten through sixth grade.

A bill in Oregon that would prohibit any discussion on sexual identity for grades kindergarten through third grade without parental notification and consent.

Legislation in Alaska that would require parental notification two weeks prior to 'any activity, class or program that includes content involving gender identity, human reproduction or sexual matters is provided to a child.'

Multiple bills in Florida that seek to double down on last year's legislation, including one that requires instruction that 'sex is determined by biology and reproductive function at birth' and another that prohibits requirements for employees to use pronouns that do not correspond with a student's sex."

---

3 Mizelle, Shawna. "In Wake of Florida Law, Additional States Seek to Restrict Certain LGBTQ Discussions in Schools | CNN Politics." *CNN, Cable News Network, 18 Mar. 2023, www.cnn.com/2023/03/18/politics/lgbtq-school-discussions/index.html.*

Being a member of this community, each of these items has the sharp sting of an individual stab at one's identity, wholeness and character.

I remember when I navigated my own sexuality. I attended a high school that had an "abstinence only" policy, meaning safe sexual practices and anything other than abstinence were removed from the table. Some friends and I created a GSA, a gay students alliance, as well as enrolled in a program to become peer sex counselors. We were donned with special backpacks that served as secret code to other students that said they could come to us if they were in need of condoms, literature and any other safe sex materials. The meetings for both organizations were held off campus, and the secretive nature behind it all automatically brought on an added layer of shame and guilt.

Many young children and teenagers do not feel they have a safe environment at home where they can openly discuss their feelings of sexual orientation and gender. School for many is a safe place where they can explore, talk to peers and find community outside of their home. When legislation is presented to prevent topics such as these, the guilt these individuals feel can be intensified when they are now associated with the severity of breaking a law.

Often, a right to life is discussed when it comes to women's rights and pregnancy and abortion access. I take it one step forward by saying a right to life for everyone is the right to live freely, to be accepted for all you are and to find and establish community with like-minded individuals. When legislation such as this is passed, it removes this ability from individuals of the LGBTQIA community.

When individuals who have opinions that are discriminatory toward those in the LGBTQIA community, they should question how they would feel if any part of their identity was used to prevent their equal treatment and inclusion in any environment. Everyone is entitled to their own opinions, but more so, each and every individual deserves the right to feel free in being their true and authentic selves.

Theresa Bernesser is a 35-year-old lesbian residing in the Western North Carolina mountain region. She dedicates herself to trying to make a lasting impact on her corner of the world by approaching individuals from all walks of life with an open, non-judgmental and compassionate attitude. She is fueled by comedy and coffee. She shares a home with her beautiful wife and their two fur babies.

EMBRACING BOTH MY FAITH AND MY QUEERNESS

by Naiomi Gonzalez

I am a queer, nonbinary brown Puerto Rican living in the United States. I am also a devout Christian. For too many people, being nonbinary and queer are viewed as being in direct opposition to Christianity. Many of my Christian peers are on the forefront of crafting and supporting legislation that dehumanizes queer and trans people and that seeks to strip people like me of my right to marry and to express my gender identity. Many of my fellow Christians equate being queer and nonbinary with being a predator and seek to criminalize being part of the LGBTQIA+ community.

However, while some Christians have used their faith to justify attempts at silencing queer and trans people, my Christian faith inspires me to fully embrace and delight in my queerness. My Christian faith pushes me to advocate for the marginalized and vulnerable and to create a country where the rights of all are respected. My Christian faith rejects the imposition of a theocracy and instead embraces the diversity of religious faith and human experiences. The loudest voices within American Christianity may be those seeking to attack LGBTQIA+ rights, but they aren't the only voices. My voice matters.

My Experience as a Queer, Nonbinary Christian in the US—the Bad and the Ugly

It seems as if everywhere I turn, both online and in the "real" world, I am confronted by the reality that many of my Christian peers view me as less than human because I do not fit into the gender norms that they consider to be God-ordained. I am frequently exposed to language that dehumanizes me and treats me as an abomination to be eradicated.

On social media, I am constantly told that I am "disobeying God" and that my insistence that queer and trans people are beloved children of God is a distortion of Christianity.

I have been subject to death threats, with one of my fellow Christians going so far as to want to "hunt me down." To be sure, most Christians I have interacted with online and in person eschew threats of physical violence and instead warn me that I am going to spend an eternity burning in hell if I do not repent. Despite having a Master's in Divinity from an accredited seminary, my knowledge of the Bible and Christian history are called into question on a daily basis.

I wish I could simply say that these comments are the cruel words of a handful of trolls online, but the reality is, many politicians are justifying their anti-LGBTQIA+ legislation by referencing their faith. Take for example, Rep. Gary Click, R-Vickery, who is sponsoring Ohio's "Save Adolescents from Experimentation Act or SAFE Act," which would prevent health care providers in the state from providing gender-affirming care, including puberty blockers and hormone therapy, to trans youth.

While Rep. Click claims that there are no religious motivations behind his sponsorship of the bill, a four-year-old sermon he gave has resurfaced. In the sermon in reference to trans people, he states: "God's not going to curse you in the wrong body. He's not going to curse you with desires that cannot be adequately and appropriately and biologically fulfilled correctly."[4] In the sermon, Rep. Click also endorses conversion therapy which seeks to change a person's sexual orientation, gender identity, or gender expression.

Conversion therapy is known to have negative physical and mental ramifications for those subjugated to it. Victor Madrigal-Borloz, an independent expert for the UN on sexual orientation and gender speaking at the Human Rights Council in 2020, described the lasting harm that conversion therapy causes:

"Practices of conversion therapy are not only ineffective, but they can also be extremely harmful...The combined effects of feeling powerless and extreme humiliation generate profound feelings of shame, guilt, self-disgust and worthlessness, which can

---

4 Riley Roliff, Ohio Capital Journal May 24. "Sponsor of Ohio Trans Youth Health Care Ban Claims No Religious Motive. Sermon Suggests Otherwise." Ohio Capital Journal, May 24, 2023. https://ohiocapitaljournal.com/2023/05/24/sponsor-of-ohio-trans-youth-health-care-ban-claims-no-religious-motive-sermon-suggests-otherwise/.

result in a damaged self-concept and enduring personality changes."[5]

That feeling of helplessness and humiliation hits close to home. While I never experienced formal conversion therapy, I grew up attending a church that viewed same sex attraction and being trans and nonbinary has an affront to God. During my formative teenage years, I repeatedly heard sermons stating those who "acted on" their same sex attraction would be subject to an eternity of hellfire. Being a Christian and a member of the LGBTQIA+ community was viewed as incompatible and anyone who believed otherwise was believed to be a tool of Satan to destroy Christianity.

My Childhood

I also remember vividly the pastor mocking "men who dress like women and women who dressed like men." In fact, a core part of our theology relied on gender rigid norms. In that

5 "Conversion Therapy' Can Amount to Torture and Should Be Banned Says UN Expert." OHCHR, July 13, 2020. https://www.ohchr.org/en/stories/2020/07/conversion-therapy-can-amount-torture-and-should-be-banned-says-un-expert.

church, women had to have long hair and wear long skirts, both for modesty purposes and to ensure men did not "stumble" in their faith as a result of lusting over our bodies. It was also a physical representation of the different roles men and women had in society. Women were supposed to be submissive toward their fathers and husbands. Men were to wear pants, keep their hair short and eschew any jewelry that was feminine. Rings, especially marriage rings were ok, but men who wore makeup or dared wear an earring were viewed with suspicion.

I tried my best to be the perfect, good Christian girl. I kept my hair long, even though brushing and caring for my thick, frizzy hair was a nightmare. I wore long skirts, even when they made walking difficult. More importantly, I prayed for God to take away my attraction to women. I prayed God would send me a good cisgender husband. I prayed God would make me a good and faithful woman to a good and faithful man.

But no matter how hard I prayed, I still found myself attracted to women. And I absolutely despised dressing like a "good Christian woman." I hated wearing skirts and tended to get yelled at for "sitting like a man" with my legs open and accidently showing off my granny panties.

I tried to fake it until I made it. I was assured that God would reward me for following "his" ways (God was always identified with male pronouns) and denying Satan's temptations. But as I continued to deny who I was, my shame grew, which contributed to my struggles with depression and suicidal thoughts. These thoughts were dismissed as Satan trying to attack me for following God. I was told on a consistent basis that my identity was shameful and an abomination to God. But it never occurred to the adults in my life to examine how being repeatedly told I was an abomination to God could contribute to my struggles with mental health.

Breaking Free and Embracing Who I Am

Unfortunately, I spent almost all of my teenage years believing that there was something inherently wrong and broken with me. It was only when I was a junior in high school that I finally decided that I could not pretend to be someone I was not. During a religious ethics class, I chose "homosexuality and Christianity" as the topic for my research project. (Homosexual was term was the term used back then). I was shocked to discover that there were people who were both part of the LGBTQIA+ community and still considered themselves Christian. I even learned that the Metropolitan Community Church, United Church of Christ, and the US Episcopal Church ordained as clergy those who were openly part of the LGBTQIA+ community.

That research project led me to leave behind anti-LGBTQIA+ forms of Christianity, and during my time in college and seminary, I was exposed to the idea of Christianity not only as affirming members of the LGBTQIA+ community but also as advocating for justice and equality.

LGBTQIA+ affirming Christians are often accused by unaffirming Christians of distorting the Bible and only "picking and choosing" Bible verses. But in seminary, I learned that the Bible is a vast, complicated library of books written over the span of thousands of years with hundreds of hands who wrote, rewrote, translated, edited, and compiled the various books.

I also discovered that in practice everyone picks and chooses which Bible verses to emphasize and which interpretation to embrace. The idea of taking the whole Bible literally all the time might be a nice one, but the reality is that just as the original writers, compilers, and editors were all influenced by their historical, political, and social environments, us modern day readers are as well. We just aren't always honest about the ways in which our own biases and prejudices influence our reading of the text. Take for example, the handful of Bible verses that are portrayed as "clearly" condemning the LGBTQIA+ community. When explored in their larger contexts, one recognizes they are not, in fact, condemning queer people.

For instance, the story of Sodom and Gomorrah in Genesis 19 is often used as evidence of God's wrath towards members of the LGBTQIA+ community. But most scholars argue that the sin of Sodom and Gomorrah was inhospitality and assault. Dr. Pete Enns, founder of *The Bible for Normal People*, who received his Ph.D. in Near Eastern Languages and Civilizations from Harvard University explains, "What happened in Sodom and Gomorrah was about dominance through shaming...they wanted to subjugate and humiliated these foreigners and put them in their place. God did not destroy Sodom and Gomorrah because the men were gay but for their general reputation for violence and sinfulness."[6]

In addition, for the handful of Scripture verses that some have misinterpreted as being against LGBTQIA+ quotes, there are hundreds of passages portraying God as being with the marginalized and oppressed. The Prophetic Books in the Hebrew Bible (Old Testament) speak of a God whose wrath is brought by those who exploit the marginalized: the poor, the widowed, the orphaned. One of the more well-known stories in the gospels is Jesus' quoting of Isaiah 61:

"The Spirit of the Lord is upon me,
because he has anointed me
to proclaim good news to the poor.
He has sent me to proclaim liberty to the captives
and recovering of sight to the blind,
to set at liberty those who are oppressed,
to proclaim the year of the Lord's favor."

6 Enns, Pete. "Did God Destroy Sodom and Gomorrah Because of Gay People? With Pete Enns.: By the Bible for Normal People." Facebook, May 24, 2022. https://www.facebook.com/thebiblefornormalpeople/videos/did-god-destroy-sodom-and-gomorrah-because-of-gay-people-with-pete-enns/387359703152198.

This verse has been interpreted as referring to spiritual freedom. However, the gospels portray a Jesus who cares about the material conditions of the marginalized in the here and now. Jesus preached a liberation in the here and now.

Recognizing the complexity of the Bible as well as the overwhelming number of verses that proclaim a God who sides with the marginalized, helped me to recognize that my queerness is not, in fact, an abomination. God made me queer and nonbinary and delights in me. Moreover, my faith inspires me to push back against the harmful legislation being passed to strip members of the LGBTQIA+ community of our rights. Many times, Christian language is used to justify these horrific laws. But the fact of the matter is that these politicians do not speak for all Christians. They do not speak for me.

Naiomi Gonzalez (she/they) is a professional nerd. They have a BA in Religious Studies from Moravian College (Now Moravian University), an M. Div from Brite Divinity School, an MA in Middle Eastern and Islamic Studies from George Mason University, and an MA in History from Texas Christian University. They are passionate about advocating for a Christianity that is liberative and that challenges oppression and injustice. Their writing can be found at: https://faithfullyradicalchristian.substack.com/

DEAR WHITE CHURCH

by Dr. Olga Pahom

Dear White Church,

I am the immigrant in your midst.

And I've been struggling.

You once welcomed me in and befriended me. You cared for me when I arrived here with nothing but a bag of clothes. You became the family I did not have in a foreign land. You sent me to college. You gave me a wedding. You supported me and prayed for me when I worked in foreign lands. You visited me when I was in the hospital. You brought me chicken casserole and lemon cake when my babies were born. I will never forget the love and the kindness you have shown me.

You once introduced me to Jesus. You taught me that he loves me, an immigrant, as much as he loves you. You sing to my half-Mexican children: "Jesus loves the little children, all the children of the world, any color dark or light, they are precious in his sight. Jesus loves the little children of the world."

You once encouraged me to read the Bible to get to know God better. You shared many Bible verses with me over the years, including these:

When a foreigner resides among you in your land, do not mistreat them. The foreigner residing among you must be treated as your native-born. Love them as you love yourself, for you were foreigners in Egypt. I am the Lord your God. (Leviticus 19:33-34)

I was hungry and you gave me something to eat, I was thirsty and you gave me something to drink, I was a stranger and you invited me in, I needed clothes and you clothed me, I was sick and you looked after me, I was in prison and you came to visit me. Truly I tell you, whatever you did for one of the least of these brothers and sisters of mine, you did for me. (Matthew 25:35-36, 40)

Whoever claims to love God yet hates a brother or sister is a liar. For whoever does not love their brother and sister, whom they have seen, cannot love God, whom they have not seen. (1 John 4:20)

You once taught me that God delights in truth spoken in love, in actions that match our words, and in faithfulness and integrity.

Remember?

I will always remember how you showed up in my life.

But I also can't forget how you showed up during the 2016 and 2020 presidential elections. And how you showed up for the last state and local elections. Even after Uvalde, El Paso, and Santa Fe. How you supported and cheered white supremacists running for office even as they openly insulted and humiliated immigrants and minorities. How you praised them on social media. How you held them up as great leaders who are fit to shape my son's ideas about what it means to be a man and my daughter's ideas about what it means to be a woman. How you vocally and enthusiastically rally behind leaders whose words and actions embody the opposite of everything you taught me, the opposite of what Jesus and the apostles taught, lived, and died for.

Leaders whose words and actions are not loving, truthful, or faithful.

Leaders who say that Mexican men like my husband are "bad hombres" and "rapists" who bring crime, drugs, and problems to the U.S.

Leaders who call women like me names so base and demeaning that I do not want to repeat them.

Leaders who say that my friends of diverse backgrounds and faiths have no place here, unless they are Christian and white.

Leaders endorsed by the Ku Klux Klan.

At first, I was shocked to discover that you overwhelmingly support these leaders. You were a significant part of the [not so] silent majority in 2016 and in 2020, contributing to making racism, xenophobia, and misogyny the new normal.

What happened to "Jesus *loves* ALL the children of the world"?

I once heard you saying that you believed that.

I once saw you living that.

I thought you meant that.

I thought I knew you.

I am not so sure anymore.

If you say that you believe one thing but vocally or silently support the opposite way, who are you?

Does this mean that you have always mistrusted or hated people like me?

Did you perform acts of service towards me out of true love or out of religious duty?

Do you believe that God is more concerned about the wellbeing of white Christians than about the wellbeing of Hispanics, African

Americans, Muslims, and other categories of "others"?

I thought I knew you.

I am not so sure anymore.

Your overwhelming silent, as well as your enthusiastically loud support for prejudice against immigrants and minorities is tearing down your sisters and brothers. It's tearing down God's vision of mercy and justice that you once convinced me to embrace.

You may say that you do not endorse political or religious leaders *because* of their prejudice against immigrants but *despite* it. This means that certain *issues* are more important to you than certain *people*.

People like me.

People like my husband.

People like my children.

People like my friends.

People who are not white and Christian.

People created in the image of God.

The Bible you taught me to love tells how religious people consistently tested if Jesus was on the right side of *the issues* (taxes, holidays, sin hierarchies, interpretation of scriptures, and others). I see Jesus consistently lifting *people* above *issues* and choosing *love* over the right position on controversial topics. Love seems to be the only right stance on any issue for him.

The Bible you gave me at my baptism says God desires mercy, not sacrifice (Hosea 6:6), but I feel sacrificed on the altar of *issues*.

Next time I see you, and you smile, hug me, and tell me I am welcome, do you mean it or are you just being nice?

Do you really love me, or do you mistrust or hate me?

Am I more important to you than *the issues*?

I am not so sure anymore.

I love Jesus and I will be committed to him for the rest of my life thanks to the love, hospitality, generosity, goodness, and kindness you once showed me. I will be eternally grateful to you for pointing me to the man still walking the dusty, unpopular roads of religion and beckoning people to leave the issues behind, follow him, love others, welcoming "the other" even if it means giving up privilege and embracing persecution.

I thought that when it came to leaders, this is the man you wanted to follow.

I thought I knew you.

I am not so sure anymore.

I pray to find the brown Middle Eastern carpenter in your midst once again.

Dr. Olga Pahom serves as Associate Professor of Linguistics and Cultural Studies and Associate Dean of the Honors College at Lubbock Christian University. She holds a Ph.D. in English with a Linguistics Concentration and an M.A. in Applied Linguistics from Texas Tech University. Her academic work focuses on intercultural communication, bilingualism, gender and language, and second language acquisition. She is an immigrant from Moldova and frequently writes and gives talks on issues related to language, culture, immigration, and faith.

BEHEADING AND SILENCING OF THE POWERFUL WOMAN

by Laura Holt

When we talk about the beheading of Medusa by Perseus, we're not just talking about the physical slaying. While the act in itself is gruesome and violent and speaks volumes to the bloodlust and hatred patriarchal men have toward powerful women, as well as the lengths they are willing to go to prevent women from keeping that power, there's a second layer to it that's equally as important. And that is the silencing of women of power.

In order to decapitate someone, either by a hand-held blade like an executioner's ax or a more mechanized weapon like a guillotine, the head must be completely severed from the body at the neck. When this happens, the vocal cords, which are located below the epiglottis, are also severed. In other words, remove the head, and the mouth is no longer connected to the voice box.

Not surprisingly, this was a popular form of execution throughout history. In April of 1550, a Swedish woman by the name of Lasses Birgitta was convicted of using sorcery to raise the dead and beheaded for her supposed crimes. This act sparked the Torsåker witch trials, the largest witch trials in Swedish history, where no fewer than 71 people (65 of whom were women) were beheaded and then burned to prevent their corpses from rising again and cursing their executioners.

In May of 1536, Anne Boleyn, Queen of England and the second wife of Henry VIII, was beheaded for the crimes of adultery, incest, and plotting to kill her husband, the king. Modern historians, however, note that there was no substantial evidence to purport these accusations. Rather, they hold to the popular theory that Anne, being well-educated, outspoken, opinionated, and temperamental, did not live up to Henry's idea of what a good wife should be. Not only had she refused to become his mistress and insisted that he marry her before she would sleep with him, leading to Henry's eventual split with the Catholic church, which refused to annul his marriage with his first wife, Catherine, and thereby making her indirectly responsible for the rise of the Protestant church in England and subsequently unpopular with much of the English population. She was also only able to bear him a daughter rather than the son he needed to succeed him on the throne, and in those times, it was believed the woman was directly responsible for the sex of the child, not the man as science has since proven. With her dead, he would be free to marry his newest love interest, Jane Seymour, and hopefully gain the heir he desired as well as win back the goodwill of the people and the church.

In October of 1793, Marie Antoinette, wife of Louis XVI and Queen of France, was also beheaded for crimes of high treason. However, like the English Anne, there is much debate among modern historians as to what, if any, Marie's crimes may have been. As a foreigner, she was never very popular with the people of France. When the rise of the printing press led to the publication of political pamphlets that served only to slander royals like Antoinette, false accusations and rumors spread through the streets like wildfire. By the time the Revolution began, she had been blamed for everything from promiscuity and harboring sympathies for France's enemies to being directly responsible for the country's financial deficits due to her lavish spending. Some propose these libelles, as they were called, were even where the "Let them eat cake" quote that is so popularly associated with Marie today arose from, though there is no hard evidence to support the theory. The earliest known documented version of this quote comes from Jean-Jacques Rousseau's *Les Confessions*, who references having heard of an unnamed princess's solution to being told the peasants had no bread, although here it reads "Let them eat brioche." Either way, the French people clearly considered Marie's death as a necessary step toward achieving freedom, and her execution was seen by many as a symbol that the revolution had done what it was meant to despite the negative effect the revolution had on the country's already weakened financial state.

By beheading women who held either supposed or actual positions of power, men throughout history were not only slaying the witch or the monster, so to speak. They were effectively silencing her at the same time, thus preventing her from speaking out or using her power against what they considered the dominant male species. The voice has always been seen as a thing of power, and therefore, a woman's voice is a thing to be feared and controlled by men lest it be used against them. In ancient societies, Puritan New England society, and even modern society, women are still being silenced one way or the other. How many of us have been told that we sound too emotional, too shrill, too dramatic when we speak about a subject which we are passionate about? And how many of us have reacted with silence, embarrassment, in response to those statements?

As Kristen J. Sollee writes in *Witches, Sluts, Feminists*, "In New England witchcraft accusations...the witch's speech revealed the full destructive power of the female voice. The witch's cursing, the demoniac's roaring: These were the ultimate ravages of women's words left unchecked. The 'right' kind of woman would never speak thusly. Famed New England Minister Cotton Mather—a notorious supporter of the Salem trials—wrote at length about proper linguistic deportment for proper women in 1692. It was best to hold one's tongue, be soft spoken, and think before you speak. 'Tis the Whore, that is clamorous,' Mather declared. Women's language is similarly policed today. We are told that raising the pitch at the end of our sentences (uptalk) and speaking from the low, creaky spot in our larynx (vocal fry) makes us seem ditsy and immature. We are told that if we say 'sorry' too much, it makes us sound weak. We are told that if we use words such as 'like' or 'um' or 'just' (filler words) we are undercutting our own intelligence and betraying a lack of confidence in our own ideas. And yet, female speech can be a space of resistance."

Femicide—the killing of women because of their gender—has long been an issue in Turkey. In 2019 alone, nearly 300 women were killed according to the Istanbul-based group We Will Stop Femicide and more than 2,600 women since 2010. "Men can't accept that Turkey is a modern country where women have rights," says Fidan Ataselim, the group's general secretary, in an interview with NPR World. "Some of these men don't even think we have the right to live." In the same interview, Fatmagul Berktay, a professor of political science at Istanbul University, explains why this is. "Male honor depends on women's obedience and men's control of women's sexuality. It can be a daughter, it can be a wife, it can even be their own mother. If they disobey him, he is emasculated."

As Mary Beard writes in *Women and Power: A Manifesto*, "I've talked before about the ways women get silenced in public discourse. And there's plenty of that silencing still going on. We need only think of Elizabeth Warren being prevented a few weeks ago from reading out a letter by Coretta Scott King in the US Senate. What was extraordinary on that occasion wasn't only that she was silenced and formally excluded from the debate (I don't know enough about the rules of procedure in the Senate to have a sense of how justified, or not, that was); but that several men over the next couple of days did read the letter out and were neither excluded nor shut up. True, they were trying to support Warren. But the rules of speech that applied to her didn't appear to apply to Bernie Sanders, or the three other male senators who did the same." And we can see this male fear of the power behind the feminine voice and the subsequent silencing of women prevalent throughout mythology as well, if we know where to look.

The Little Mermaid, written by Hans Christian Anderson, is one of my favorites. Here, we see that the Little Mermaid's voice was not stolen like in the more popularized Disney film version, but her tongue was physically cut out by the sea witch. There was no getting her voice back. She relinquished her vocal power—her ability to speak, to sing, to tell the prince who she was—in exchange for human legs. By doing so, she embodies society's wish to transform all "wild" females into more quiet, docile creatures.

In Homer's *Odyssey*, you have the sirens, female creatures whose voices could lure sailors to their doom on the rocks around their island home. In Irish mythology, you have the Banshee, whose voice, if you are unfortunate enough to hear it, is seen as a sign of impending doom. And in Greek mythology, of course, you have Medusa, who is beheaded by Perseus. By doing so, the young man not only claims the power of Medusa's gaze for himself but also silences her voice once and for all when he severs her throat with his blade, thus ensuring that the only version of her story that will be told henceforth is his own.

Laura Holt is the award-winning author of the YA Star-Crossed series and *Village of Salt* and *Sorrow*. Her poetry and short fiction have been published in *Calla Press*, *Pegasus Literary Magazine*,

Ginosko Literary Journal, and the *Eber and Wein 2015 Anthology*. She is a self-professed word witch with a passion for mythology, history, and caffeine who enjoys telling stories about angry girls with magic powers and wild natures, whose bark is as bad as their bite. When she's not writing, you can find her stretched out on a yoga mat, hiking down wooded trails, or wandering the aisles at a local bookstore searching for her next great read. She lives in small-town Georgia with her daughter, three cats, and a lot of fake plants.

Follow her on Instagram to stay up to date on bookish news, events, and book and music recs, or subscribe to her monthly newsletter for even more exclusive content and writer resources.

AN AMERICAN WOMAN'S BODY

IS ONLY HER OWN WHEN CONVENIENT FOR THOSE IN POWER

by Valerie Dimino

The reasons I've been hesitant to say any of this for months have now become the very reasons I need to say it all: the topic is massive and too volatile to grab hold of, and I am afraid and frustrated and exhausted, and I am a woman and am just one voice. Yes. Please hear this one afraid, frustrated, exhausted woman's voice now and know that I am one of millions.

The overturning of *Roe v. Wade* is just the latest in a long, long line of affronts on American women's liberties, their rights to their own bodies, health, safety, and futures. It is yet another example of women being discredited about their deeply personal, often traumatic experiences and stripped of autonomy. And the long line that comes before it, of course, makes this latest step not more trivial but more devastating. It highlights that there are many battles still to fight.

I was brought into one such battle about eight years ago, when a friend introduced me to a young woman named Jessica. My friend told me Jessica had been through some things that they'd both long thought would make a powerful book, and she asked if I'd want to meet Jessica and talk about collaborating on that book together.

The first thing that shocked me in learning Jessica's story was the betrayal layered upon her. She survived years of sexual abuse only to be ostracized by her family and community when the truth came out. The second shock was learning that she is far from alone in that type of experience.

While working on our book, *The Man Behind the Curtain: A Memoir*, I read four other memoirs that speak to such astoundingly similar themes that they are crammed full of countless Post-it notes—and I was merely skimming the surface of some of the most recent material. In hearing Jessica's story, I was appalled by the victim shaming, the criticism and casting aside, the uphill battle to be heard or believed or to have consequences brought about. And yet these other books, these other women, detail much of the same: Michelle Bowdler's *Is Rape a Crime? A Memoir, an Investigation, and a Manifesto*; Lacy Crawford's *Notes on a Silencing*; Chanel Miller's *Know My Name*; and Chessy Prout and Jenn Abelson's *I Have the Right To: A High School Survivor's Story of Sexual Assault, Justice, and Hope*.

The question at the foundation of Bowdler's book—is rape a crime?—should not even be a question; it should be hyperbolic. But it is all too real. She writes, "Can we really say that rape is a crime given the way this felony is addressed by law enforcement, politicians, and the larger world? For many intractable social and political issues, progress gets measured by whether things are slightly less bad than they once were. Unfortunately, sex crimes are still placed in that category. Slight improvements to issues that never should have been tolerated are celebrated, and the deeper and pervasive issues remain untouched."

Bowdler discusses the discovery of 11,000 untested rape kits in a Detroit warehouse in 2009—evidence that was gathered meticulously from victims' traumatized bodies, in the immediate aftermath of the trauma, and then "treated like useless trash." As if those 11,000 people waiting for answers weren't already far too many, the same thing has taken place in countless other cities across the country, with total estimates as high as 400,000 untested kits. These numbers make the "discovery" of such "backlogs" (Bowdler puts these terms in quotes, too) a difficult thing to celebrate, their long-overdue processing—if even still possible—certainly a "slight improvement" at best.

One of these untested kits, in California, some six years after the Detroit discovery, was Miller's, who had been told hers would get through the process faster because of the media attention surrounding her case. (Miller is the woman Brock Turner assaulted, introduced to the world as Emily Doe, whose victim impact statement went viral.) But even Miller's rape kit sat untouched for months, hundreds waiting in line before hers. "How could that be; this was not fruit rotting, it was little pieces of us in each one, an indispensable story," Miller writes in *Know My*

Name. "It also meant there was a population of victims in my vicinity, disguised in their everyday lives, going to work, refilling their coffee, eyes wide at night, waiting."

Many of these victims want to press charges, go to trial, testify, and fight for justice but aren't able to because of issues like these, outside of their control. Miller writes about a friend who had also been assaulted and who had "called the police, completed the rape kit, but even after she did everything victims are instructed to do, she was informed it was not enough to move forward."

Many other victims, as I heard firsthand from the detectives who investigated Jessica's case, choose not to proceed to trial, so weary and discouraged from the earlier steps that they can't bear the thought of continuing. It's easy to see why, given experiences like Jessica's—who endured four years of investigation and court proceedings, largely alone, as a teenager—and experiences like Miller's, and Bowdler's, and Crawford's, and Prout's, and Anita Hill's, and Christine Blasey Ford's, and the dozens of women who have accused Donald Trump of sexual assault, and the *many thousands* of others who have had to fight for years just to be heard, let alone believed, let alone given justice.

And any one of these stories becomes even more fraught if the victim is not white, privileged, straight, or cisgender or if the victim has a physical disability, intellectual disability, or mental illness.

Each one of these victims who does share her story, in whatever form, to whatever extent she is able, is grabbing a microphone, a megaphone, an opportunity to speak these difficult truths and seek justice not only on behalf of herself but also on behalf of all these other people for whom that opportunity is never available, through no fault of their own and despite their exhausting efforts.

I lost count of the number of people I know personally who revealed to me their own stories of trauma, in varying degrees, by sharing that *The Man Behind the Curtain* would be difficult for them to read. Some haven't been ready to start it yet or may never be able to. Some have read a bit but need to take it slow. Some were nervous to read it but then felt a certain sort of comfort in hearing a story that helped them to feel seen and understood.

This sort of misery should not need company to find comfort.

As Bowdler writes, "How many more books will need to be written by victims of sex crimes describing devastating violence, the minimization that followed, and the impact both experiences have had on their lives?"

Please hear me: Women are being raped and assaulted and silenced, and then if they do summon the strength—or find themselves forced in yet another way—to speak out, they are asked, directly and behind their backs and in the public eye, why they waited so long to tell, what they are looking to gain, what they were wearing, how much they had had to drink, what specifically they had had to eat before or after consuming those drinks, etc., etc.

And now, should they find themselves pregnant from that rape, many more will be forced to bear that child.

In a country where a woman can be forced to bear a child yet be left entirely on her own to figure out how—or if—she can access healthcare for herself or the child, get leave from work to birth and care for the child, return to work and pay for childcare, find formula to feed the child, access a decent education system for the child…

In a country where massive religious networks (e.g., the Catholic church and the Southern Baptist Convention, the latter of which encompasses Jessica's family's church, which continues to revere her rapist and tried for years to cleanse the sin out of *her*) are willing and able to cover up decades of sexual abuse, committed by and concealed by the highest ranks, silencing and shaming victims on an enormous, systemic scale…

In a country where a pastor can make a careful partial confession of adultery, then be corrected publicly by his victim that it was *rape*, that she had been a *teenager*, and still he is surrounded in prayers and hugs…

In a country where "the land of the free" has more and more asterisks after it…

In a country where it feels increasingly like those in power do not want to be inconvenienced by our voices…

I implore you to keep sharing your stories, to keep asking the difficult questions, to keep seeking truth, to keep listening.

In response to continued and exponentially aggressive attempts at silencing, I implore you to keep speaking up. Louder.

Valerie Dimino is the coauthor of the memoir *The Man Behind the Curtain*. She has been passionate about writing since kindergarten, when she wrote and illustrated her first short story in marker. Holding bachelor's and master's degrees in creative writing from SUNY Brockport, she has 15 years of professional writing, editing, and marketing experience in the fields of higher education, performing arts, and medical informatics. She lives in Lakeville, New York, with her fiancé, Rich. She blogs and shares more of her writing life at valeriedimino.com. Connect with her on Instagram at @valeriedimino.

TIC FREELY

by Hannah Noblewolf

When I was packing to move last summer, I found an old diary of mine. I kept it on and off from 8th grade to 10th grade, and in it, I wrote with the sincerity and certainty only a young teenager can—about my crush, about my dreams, about fights with my family and friends. Flipping through the pages, it was a strange feeling—almost nostalgic but not quite. Middle and high school were objectively the worst times of my life. It was more that I felt a melancholy compassion for the young girl I remembered on the other side of the page. I was awkward, unsure, coming to terms with my sexuality and desperate to get out of a small New England town where I felt I would never be welcomed. It didn't feel like me, even though I knew it was.

Some of the entries were more standard diary entries, some pages were full of doodles, and some were bad poems. The further I got in the diary, the more my distant empathy for the author became concern. It eventually morphed into a disgusting feeling that sat in the pit of my stomach like lead. I still can't articulate what I felt looking at the hurried writing of my past self—the closest feeling I could identify would be revulsion or dread. One entry actually made my hands begin to shake, one from less than 6 months after I got my diagnosis of Tourette Syndrome.

It's been well over 10 years since my diagnosis, and I've likely explained it thousands of times in different ways.

"Tourette Syndrome is a neurological condition characterized by repetitive, involuntary movements or sounds. The movements and sounds that I make are called tics. It's believed to be a genetic condition, and there is no cure. I would appreciate your patience. I know it can be disruptive."

"I have a neurological condition."

"I am not having a seizure, I have Tourette's, I don't need an ambulance."

It was my best friend who noticed my tics first. I don't remember when they started, but I do vividly remember coming home from school one day with my two close friends, Angel and Sarah. We were standing by the entrance to the kitchen, talking about what to do. My mother came in behind us. She asked me what I was doing. I had no idea what she was talking about.

"That shoulder thing, what are you doing? Quit it."

I was still confused, but once my attention had been drawn to it, I noticed my right shoulder jerking back slightly, over and over. I knew I wasn't doing it, so how could I stop it? Before I could panic or my mother could get more frustrated with me, I heard Angel from behind me.

"She's been doing that for months. You haven't noticed?"

That was the beginning of a blurry nightmare. I was referred to a neurologist, who believed that 12 was too old for Tourette Syndrome to present for the first time. I don't know if it was the case with him, but I've heard from other people with neurological disorders that some neurologists don't believe girls can have TS, just because it impacts boys more frequently. This is blatantly untrue, and I found out years later that I had an almost textbook presentation. Sometimes I wonder if my neurologist genuinely couldn't see how scared I was, or if he just didn't care.

He made it clear that his opinion was that I was doing it for attention. He did agree to run tests to cover all the bases in the event I wasn't faking. I had EKGs, an MRI, and more blood draws than I can count. Eventually, he told my father it was a transient tic disorder and they'd be gone within six months. Safe to say, it's been a little longer than six months at this point.

I had a solid four years of hell. My tics got increasingly worse. I developed OCD, generalized anxiety disorder, and major depressive disorder—all common co-occurring conditions of TS. That same neurologist put me on benzodiazepines as a 12-year-old with a family history of drug addiction. I tried CBT but it caused me too much physical and emotional distress to try to counter my tics, so we eventually moved on to heavier medications. I felt like I was bobbing in the ocean, like I'd come up for air once in a while, only to be dragged back under the next time I was medicated.

The most upsetting thing, the thing I couldn't gloss over when I read that diary entry again, was the complete sense of betrayal. Betrayal by my own body. I've never experienced a greater fear than when I realized that this was forever.

TS is incurable. I would *never* be fully in control of my body again.

I tried to process it a few different ways. For a brief period as a teenager, when I was still coming to terms with my diagnosis, I would say I was grateful that it was me dealing with this, because it meant someone else wasn't suffering, and I could handle it. I didn't handle it—I developed a benzo dependency and began to self-harm to numb that feeling rather than admit that *I* was suffering.

Then I leaned hard into aggressive positivity. "I'm different, but that means I just make the world more colorful." During this period, I was hospitalized for anxiety and suicidal ideation twice, because I didn't *want* to make the world more colorful; I wanted it all to stop, at all costs.

In college, when my tics were still ever-present but no longer controlling my life, I acknowledged them when I needed to, and I warned my classes at the beginning of each semester out of courtesy. The older I got, the more I wanted to pretend it didn't exist. That I was neurotypical. I learned how to suppress my tics for longer periods and to manipulate other muscles to make tics less noticeable or offensive to others.

When I think about it in the abstract, it's easy for me to talk about my disability like it doesn't impact my life in a meaningful way. Sometimes it's easier. It's certainly easier for the people asking me questions. My concern has always been for others. I don't want to upset them. I don't want them to pity me or infantilize me. I feel like a burden when I talk about it honestly. I'm "disruptive" when I tic in public, and it makes people uncomfortable. Sitting on the floor of my shitty one-bedroom apartment, packing my old diary away, I had a thought for the first time. Why did I do all of this? Why was I still doing all of this?

There was a documentary from 2005, called *I Have Tourette's but Tourette's Doesn't Have Me*. That is, in all honesty, complete bullshit. It is literally how my brain is wired, similar to autism. TS may not control my life entirely, but it is a huge factor in how I move through the world. American culture values the ideas of self-determinism and individualism above all else. We like to pretend that willpower is enough to overcome any hurdle. That whole, "pull yourself up by your bootstraps" nonsense. Individuals are responsible for everything that goes on in their lives—good things are earned, as well as bad things. *This* is why the general population loves seeing trauma porn of disabled people. It's proof to them that we earned what we have. By the same logic, disabled people that can't "overcome adversity" and do everything able-bodied neurotypicals can just didn't try hard enough. The results of a cosmic meritocracy. It is also why I have never been fully honest about what it's like living in a body that doesn't always feel like my own anymore. If I'm honest, I'm admitting I can't do everything on my own and that's a moral failing in our society. It's permission to be treated like a child or discarded.

So let me stop lying. I am disabled. I am not "differently abled." I have to always be cognizant of my triggers and avoid them. I have to do constant mental math to determine how much stress I can tolerate before my tics get bad. It's true that tics themselves don't hurt, but my body aches constantly from the repetitive motions I've been making involuntarily and constantly for over half my life. My throat hurts when I try to disguise my vocal tics, so my swearing doesn't get me dirty looks or cause a confrontation in public. I suppress my tics even around long-term partners, because I'm scared they'll think I'm broken. After this long, the only people I don't automatically suppress them around are my siblings, who have tic disorders themselves. Even when I do everything "right," I'll occasionally have tic attacks that keep me up at night, and I feel like a failure. I stare at the ceiling, trying to leave my body, feeling like I should be able to power through the shortcomings of my nervous system. I miss being able bodied, frequently.

All of this being said, my TS hasn't taken my joy permanently. I love baking and watching bad B-horror movies. I can still go to a park on a hot day and eat ice cream with my friends. On cold nights, I like curling up by a warm fireplace with someone I love and watching the fire until it dies. I'm a passionate anthropologist pursuing my Ph.D. I like studying with my cat in the room, even if I have to stop every five minutes to wrestle my sticky notes out of her mouth or steal my pens back. I still have things I want to do. I want to travel and to be there for the important moments in my little siblings' lives. I want to have children.

That last point in particular has caused a few arguments in my life. Tourette Syndrome doesn't have any specific known cause, but it is believed to have a strong genetic component. Yes, I will readily admit that having TS has made my life more difficult. I don't think that that's entirely the result of my TS, though. The more I think about it, a large amount of my issues come from living in a world that actively prevents disabled people from living our lives fully. All of the concessions we make to keep others comfortable and to fit into the cultural framework we've been shoved into. I shouldn't have to hide my lived reality to keep others happy at the cost of my happiness.

The Tourette Association of America's current slogan is #TicFreely. When I first saw it on their social media, I rolled my eyes a little. Sure, that was fine for other people, but what about me? I really have never believed that it was an option for me to just…be. To be open and honest that yeah, it *is* tough sometimes to be neurodivergent, to make dumb jokes about my tics, to maybe even learn to not be afraid of my own body anymore. The more I've sat on it, the more I realize that it could be possible. My life is worth living, as is. If my future child has TS, their life will be worth living too. Maybe if I speak my truth without worrying about my existence as a disabled person offending people, I can be the adult that I needed as a scared little girl trying to figure out how to navigate life after having something I took for granted ripped away from me. I hope that one day I can open up that diary and read that entry again, knowing that I've healed and I'm not hiding from myself or making myself smaller for the sake of others.

Hannah Noblewolf (she/they) is a queer 26-year-old cultural-linguistic anthropology doctoral candidate from Western Massachusetts. Her passions include baking, cryptids, reproductive justice, and treating her grown cat like a baby.

WITHOUT CONTEXT:

GROWING UP ADOPTED

by C.J. Abraham

When I look in the mirror, I'm not sure what I see. It's me, and I know that, but I don't know who or what "me" is. Until I gave birth to my first child, I'd never looked into the face of someone who shared my DNA, someone who looked like me. The power of that moment didn't escape me, as I remember uttering in awe, "I look just like her." The first frame of reference I had for my own face was in the face of a seconds-old infant. Without the foundation of our genetic history ("I have my mother's eyes, my father's nose," etc.), we are looking at ourselves completely out of context, and it's clear sometimes that society sees us that way as well.

"You're so lucky."

"You should be thankful."

"Your adoptive parents saved you."

These are things adoptees hear daily, and they significantly undercut a tremendous part of the adoptee experience: grief. Adoption, by its very nature, is an institution founded upon loss—loss for the adoptive parents that can't bear children, loss for the expectant parent who can't afford to raise their child, loss for the adoptee who is signed away to strangers, and sometimes it feels as though every corner brings a subsequent loss when growing up adopted. Loss of identity. Loss of one's birth culture. Loss of one's original name. Loss of connection to one's genetic history and genetic mirrors. The list goes on and on. Yet, in society, all we hear are the echoing praises of the practice, "You should be grateful." Sometimes, I want to yell into space, "Grateful for what? For the complete loss of self that occurred as a transaction when I was just days old? For the loss of my first mom at birth and then again when she passed before we could meet?" I am not grateful. I am grieving. Grieving, alongside thousands of other adoptees, a life of loss that society doesn't recognize, grieving a loss of self that is inexplicable to others who haven't experienced it themselves, and experiencing it all alone whilst trying to cater to society's expectations for adoptees—be quiet, be thankful, be happy.

After reading about adoption and loss, it should come as no surprise that adoptees are significantly overrepresented in mental health settings. Simply being adopted doubles the likelihood of working with a mental health professional. However, few mental health professionals are trained in working with adoptees (many are experienced with adoptive parents or families, but few are attuned to the unique needs of adoptees themselves), leaving adoptees overrepresented and underserved. I personally started therapy sometime in middle school, and through years of working with multiple mental health professionals, not one of them ever mentioned to me that what I was experiencing may have been connected to the fact that I was adopted. In my early thirties, I began to work with an adoption competent mental health provider, and the difference was astounding. Still, through all I've learned about myself and the impact my relinquishment and adoption had on me, I find it is almost impossible to have a conversation about adoption-connected trauma in mixed audiences. Society is so attached to the narrative of adoption as a positive event to be celebrated, that I find most people are put off by hearing about the negative impact it can (and often does) have on adoptee mental health. Society looks at adoptees and sees children saved from unimaginable lives, blank slates, effortlessly assimilated into their adoptive families, free of the burdens that lead us there- yet again and again, when speaking with adoptees, it is clear that this is just not the case, demonstrating yet another way that adoptees are decontextualized within our own worlds.

Another way adoptees are forced to live in a reality different than most is that many states deny adoptees access to their original birth certificates. Denying individuals the right to know our own origins and biological identities perpetuates a sense of disconnection and insecurity. Every person deserves the opportunity to understand their own history and heritage, which includes the right to access their authentic birth records. Additionally, the practice of forging birth certificates during the adoption process raises ethical concerns. By replacing a child's original birth certificate with an altered version, it erases a vital piece of our identity. This undermines the adoptee's right to accurate documentation and reinforces a system where truth is sacrificed for the convenience of others, a mindset perpetuated throughout the lives of many adoptees.

Moreover, the commodification of children within the adoption industry is deeply troubling. It reduces the value of a child to a mere transaction, emphasizing profit over the well-being and individual rights of the child. This dehumanizing perspective must be challenged, as it overlooks the importance of providing a nurturing and supportive environment for all children, regardless of their origin or adoption status. Ultimately, recognizing the rights of adoptees to access their original birth certificates, promoting transparency in the adoption process, and prioritizing the well-being of children over financial interests are essential steps towards a more equitable and ethical approach to adoption.

In conclusion, the adoptee experience is marked by profound challenges stemming from loss, grief, and a disconnection from one's genetic heritage. Society's romanticized narrative of adoption often overlooks the complex emotional impact it has on adoptees, pushing us to suppress our grief and conform to unrealistic expectations. The lack of adequate mental health support tailored to the unique needs of adoptees further exacerbates our struggle, leaving us overrepresented and underserved within the mental health system. Denying adoptees access to our original birth certificates reinforces a sense of disconnection and insecurity, denying us the right to our own history and perpetuating a system where truth is compromised for the convenience of others. Furthermore, the commodification of children within the adoption industry devalues their inherent worth and prioritizes financial interests over their well-being. It is imperative that we strive towards a more compassionate and ethical adoption system that acknowledges the rights of adoptees, fosters transparency, and places the well-being of children above all else.

CJ Abraham is a domestic infant adoptee, a devoted parent, and a passionate mental health advocate. Her writing explores the intricacies of identity and advocacy, shaped by the unique perspective of adoption and her work as a mental health professional. Beyond advocacy, CJ finds joy in family moments, powerlifting, and hiking, embracing the physical and mental balance these activities offer.

INDIEGOGO SUPPORTERS

Abraham Mata
Alice Piotrowska
Christina Meeks
Deborah Todd
Eden Nitost
Holly Howat
Janet Bontrager
Jimmy Taylor
Julio Torres
Katie Turner
Lama Ibdah
Leslie Kachel
Lizette Cruz
Michele Pollard Gonzalez
Nik Mahan
Olga Pahom
Rhennie Boyle
Sam Curtis
Sandra Corbett
Sharlan Renfrow Proper
Shenai Alonge
Sherring Dartiguenave
Stephanie Balmori
Stephen Pollard
Suzanne Steve Levine
Tari Kandemiri
Zach Levine

Kelly Esparza (she/her) is a Latinx writer and editor who holds a BA in English and a BA in Creative Writing from the University of Arizona. Her short fiction, essays, and poetry have been published in various literary journals and anthologies, and in 2021, her published short story, "Destiny Says," was nominated for a Pushcart Prize. In 2022, her YA short story, "Take the Jump," made the longlist for *Voyage YA Journal*'s Anthology Contest. She also co-wrote a screenplay for a feature film at RIPKIRK Productions. Find her on Twitter: @Kelly_Esparza7 and check out her website: kellyesparza.wordpress.com.

www.ingramcontent.com/pod-product-compliance
Lightning Source LLC
Chambersburg PA
CBHW070350200726
48294CB00003B/824

* 9 7 8 1 7 3 6 2 7 0 1 3 4 *